D1743415

Opening the Door to Language Learning: bringing language learning to the wider community

Practical ideas for setting up and supporting open, resource-based and autonomous language learning in a non-formal learning context

written and edited
by
OdLL Project partners

Education and Culture

Socrates
Lingua

This project has been carried out with the support of the European Community in the framework of the Socrates Lingua 1 programme

Original English title: Opening the Door to Language Learning:
bringing language learning to the wider community
Practical ideas for setting up and supporting open, resource-based
and autonomous language learning in a non-formal learning context

First published 2005 in English by:
Drukkerij De Beurs
Langstraat 65, 2140 Antwerp (Borgerhout), Belgium
Tel: +32 (0)3 2360624 Fax: +32 (0)3 2352240
Email: info@drukkerijdebeurs.be

Design by:
Van Gorp & Verboven
Fruithoflaan 91 Bus 25, 2600 Antwerp (Berchem), Belgium
Tel +32 (0)3 8250200 Fax +32 (0)3 8253262
Email: info@vgnv.be

ISBN 1-904190-71-5

Contents

1. Introduction

This handbook contains guidance and recommendations based on the experiences of a three-year project funded by the European Community Socrates Programme, which sought to develop and test strategies for increasing access to language learning.

The Opening the Door to Language Learning (OdLL) Project aimed to encourage organisations delivering language learning (universities, colleges, schools, publishers, businesses) to develop initiatives whereby their materials and expertise could be made available to a wider and different set of learners. The OdLL Project consisted of three phases, the first two being devoted to trialling and evaluating open learning models (see Table 1: Open learning models) in seven European countries (Belgium, Hungary, Ireland, Lithuania, Spain, Sweden and the United Kingdom). The third phase consisted of evaluating these models and compiling a guide to good practice in promoting language learning, of which this publication is a key element. Additional materials created for and by the OdLL Project are available on the following website: www.opendoor2languages.net

> "It's shifting the responsibility **from the teacher to the pupil,** taking away that dependency, which is very empowering for learning"

(Learner, Opening the Door to Language Learning Project, 2004)

1.1 How to use this handbook

This handbook has been written collectively by all the OdLL Project partners and aims to be as practical as possible, providing advice and recommendations to individuals and organisations who are engaging (or who wish to engage) in activities to promote language learning or to provide opportunities for lifelong learning.

It does not provide courses or course materials. Rather, it is intended to raise awareness of some of the key areas that need to be considered when providing learning opportunities to lifelong and non-traditional language learners.

The **table of open learning models** *(see Table 1: Open learning models)* together with the case studies are intended to provide some ideas on the possible content and purpose of an open learning programme. However, the variations and combinations of models are such that there are many more possible programmes than can be detailed here.

Key recommendations listed at the beginning of each section are based on the experiences of the OdLL Project team. A full list can be found in the *Summary of key recommendations*. The questions given throughout the forthcoming sections (indicated by ❓) are to help you, the organiser, to think through the issues involved in developing open, flexible and non-traditional learning.

Section one gives a brief outline of the rationale for the OdLL Project, details of the activities carried out as part of the project and information on the learners involved.

Section two provides a step-by-step guide to the practicalities of planning and implementing an open learning programme of the type described in section one and also in the open learning models table *(see Table 1: Open learning models)*. It identifies key areas to be considered and provides a set of reflective questions and recommendations for each one. Areas covered include recruitment, publicity, funding, timetabling and working in partnership with others.

Section three considers some of the particular pedagogic issues that need to be addressed when developing an open learning programme. These include questions of learner support and motivation as well as types and modes of assessment, monitoring and evaluation.

Section four covers learning materials, which are vital elements of any language learning programme and need particular attention when learners are operating mainly outside of a traditional classroom. Areas covered include technology and the development of study packs.

Appendices contain additional information about the OdLL Project including types of independent language learning, learner profiles, and an overview of learning technologies.

Photocopiable materials such as learner profile forms, feedback forms, etc. are included and may be freely used and adapted providing the source is acknowledged.

Supplementary materials (some of which are untranslated) include materials developed by the OdLL Project for particular activities as well as an expanded set of references and weblinks. These can be found on the Project website at www.opendoor2languages.net

Table 1: Open learning models

No.	Open learning model	Description	Example 1	Example 2	Example 3
1	Distance learning • Case study 1	Any learning programme or activity that is mainly delivered and supported remotely. May include blended learning where there is some face-to-face contact.	Distance learning using Blackboard virtual learning environment (*Belgium, phase 1)	Distance learning courses delivered via email for deaf and hard-of-hearing learners, supported by face-to-face meetings (*Hungary, phase 2)	Distance learning web-based course with some face-to-face support (*Sweden, phase 1)
2	Study or conversation group • Case studies 5, 6 and 8	Largely self-managed learner groups set up to facilitate conversation practice or peer-supported study. May be led by a native speaker, language advisor or mentor.	Conversation clubs and film sessions (*Belgium, phase 2)	Study groups and drama activities, focusing on the use of audio-visual media (*Ireland, phase 2)	Virtual conversation using telephone and video conferencing (*Sweden, phase 2)
3	Learner training • Case studies 7 and 9	A structured programme or set of materials aimed at helping learners to identify skills, needs and goals. May include activities relating to self-assessment, learning strategies and use of learning materials. Can be delivered face-to-face, online or in a printed guide.	Independent learning programme to develop foreign language lecturing skills, supported by activating sessions (*Lithuania, phase 2)	Generic language reActivation sessions in local public library, supported by self-study materials and study groups (*United Kingdom, phase 2)	
4	Open access • Case study 3	Providing access to technology and learning materials either in a language resource centre, community or public space (e.g. library), or online (e.g. website, virtual learning environment)	Designing and setting up a language resource centre in the children's section of a public library (*Spain, phase 1)	Opening university resource centres to non-traditional language learners (*Ireland phase 1 and United Kingdom, phase 1)	
5	Roadshow or taster day • Case study 2	Workshop demonstrating methods and materials for particular languages or awareness raising activity to promote language learning	Language roadshow to remote areas in order to raise awareness of self-study opportunities (*Hungary, phase 1)	Taster days to promote independent learner packs, supported by consultation meetings (*Lithuania, phase 1)	
6	Language advising • Case study 4	Face-to-face or virtual meetings between teachers, advisors, mentors and learners to discuss and plan language learning. May also include help for a particular language or skill.	Language advice service (face-to-face and virtual) for parents and university students (*Spain, phase 2)		

Refers to OdLL Project partner and test phase. For further details see www.opendoor2languages.net

1.2 Background and context

The OdLL Project was conceived in response to two main issues: lack of access to language learning materials and lack of diversity of language learning opportunities available to non-traditional learners.

Access to language learning materials

Many higher educational institutions and other providers of language learning are frequently well resourced but access to their materials is often restricted to a closed group of students. Although there are many good reasons for this, there are equally compelling reasons for opening up access to cater for a more diverse group of learners, e.g. adult lifelong learners. Facilities are frequently less well used in the evenings, at weekends and in vacation times, when many adult learners would like or would be available to use them. Additionally, if educational institutions work in cooperation with other organisations the range and use of materials can be extended. This will not only promote and encourage language learning among a wider group of learners, but will enable educational institutions and other organisations to offer different and innovative learning opportunities. This not only benefits the learners themselves but also the organisations in question if the market for language learning is increased and diversified.

Diversity of learning

Many providers of language learning are skilled in the delivery of so-called traditional modes of learning, e.g. learning delivered in formal classrooms by a language teacher. Prior to the OdLL Project detailed here, there was some (mainly anecdotal) evidence that many adult learners did not favour this as a mode of learning. Reasons for this may be that they have already 'failed' as language learners in the classroom or perhaps do not wish to take assessed (certificated) courses. In the United Kingdom (where the OdLL Project was conceived) there was also evidence that many adult learners completed beginners programmes but often progressed no further in their language learning and were even repeating the beginners' stage rather than progressing to the next level. This may be due to lack of confidence, restricted availability of second-level courses, time constraints or little flexibility in the mode of learning offered.

Thus, the OdLL Project set out to explore ways in which some of these perceived concerns could be addressed. This was to be achieved by opening up access to materials and by offering a variety of open and flexible learning pathways. During the course of the OdLL Project it became clear from talking to adult learners that they had a very diverse range of reasons for learning a language (see *Appendix 2: The profile of learners*) and were looking for ways of learning that could meet these needs. These would not necessarily require certification, weekly attendance at traditional classes or a formal language course.

Below are some of the key ideas and outcomes of the Project, which have formed the basis of the guidance given elsewhere in this publication.

Learner autonomy

The OdLL Project was conceived as a means to provide greater and different learning opportunities to (mainly) adult language learners. It aimed to explore the possibilities for setting up and supporting a more learner-centred and autonomous way of language learning. Definitions of learner autonomy are varied and open to debate, but for the purposes of the OdLL Project the terms *Open learning and Supported independent learning* were used. These mainly relate to learning outside of the formal classroom or curriculum but with support and direction from a teacher, advisor, native speaker or other language expert.

More on the categories of learner autonomy identified by the OdLL Project can be found in *Appendix 1: Types of independent language learning*.

The community of learners

In summary OdLL Project learners were:
- Non-traditional learners (not registered students, i.e. not pursuing a formal course of study)
- Non-specialist language learners (who may not have studied the language formally, or for a very long time)
- Lifelong learners (adults who are balancing learning with work, family and other commitments or who are returning to learning)

Note: the OdLL Project did, in some instances, work with children where this related to a specific local need or to the particular expertise of the Project partners.

Overall 1421 learners were involved in the two test phases of the project. Data collected from the 156 phase two learners is summarised briefly below.

The most common age group was 25-34 with the smallest number of learners falling into the youngest and oldest categories (under-24 and over-55). There was a clear majority of female learners and 55% of all learners had higher education experience.

Among the most popular reasons for learning a language were:
- To be able to read books, newspapers and magazines in the target language
- To be able to use the language on holiday
- To refresh languages already studied or learnt

Some 35% also reported that they were studying languages for pleasure.

More details of the learners involved in the OdLL Project (age, gender, educational experience, language learning goals) can be found in *Appendix 2: The profile of learners.*

Language learning models

Below is a summary of the types of activities trialled during the OdLL Project. These informed the models outlined in *Table 1: Open learning models* and the recommendations given in this guide (see *Summary of key recommendations*).
- Distance and blended learning (a mixture of e-learning and face-to-face sessions) for adult learners
- Language roadshow for schools
- Open access to university language centres
- Language learning activities and materials in a public library
- Language learning study groups for adult learners
- Virtual conversation groups for adult learners
- Learner training courses for adult independent learners
- Language training for specific or professional purposes
- Language learning advice service for adults wishing to support their children's language learning
- Drama activities to support language learning
- Distance learning for hearing-impaired language learners

The results

Following each activity feedback was collected from learners (see *Photocopiable materials: Learner feedback form*) and each organiser completed an evaluative summary. From these, together with records of learner attendance, retention rates and work submitted the following benefits and barriers were identified:

Benefits for learners

- Not being obliged to do a test or examination
- Special needs addressed
- Confidence enhancement
- Motivation
- Fun
- Meeting and working with other learners
- Discovery of new materials
- Self-awareness
- Acquisition of new (transferable) skills
- Learning in a non-traditional way
- Making progress in the learning of a particular language

Benefits for Project partners

For the partners in the OdLL Project, the opportunity to explore and develop new approaches to learning was a major benefit as was the opportunity to share ideas, experiences and materials across cultures. As a result it was possible to engage in fourteen different learning experiments and to learn collectively and individually from each experience. Additionally, some colleagues were able to develop ideas and initiatives that will become embedded in future language learning provision within their organisation. They were also able to work innovatively with new partners within their own country. The experience of working in this way has been hugely rewarding both in terms of learners and partners and it is hoped that other organisations may take up some of the ideas contained in this handbook.

Barriers for learners

Needless to say there were areas of difficulty for learners owing to the type of learning being offered (learner-centred) and differing learning styles. These included:

- Time management
- Balancing learning with other commitments
- Lack of self-discipline
- Preference for traditional ways of learning
- Lack of IT skills
- Resistance to the idea of independent language learning

Barriers for Project partners

Issues that arose for those organising the learning are explored in this handbook.
These included:

- Appropriate use and cost of publicity
- Finding venues
- Timing of the learning period
- Collecting and recording data on learners
- Communicating with learners
- Assessing and monitoring progress
- Finding and working with national partners

Notwithstanding these barriers, learners (and partners) taking part in the OdLL Project were very positive in their responses to the experience. For all concerned the Project achieved its key aim of fostering greater awareness of the possibilities for, and benefits of, language learning outside the formal classroom:

"I found the experience fun and it made me realise you are **never too old** **to learn a language**"

"**Getting together** with other language learners, it's been such a **motivating** force"

"Now I feel a stronger urge **to learn more**"

"I am a **different language learner** from the person I used to be as a language learner"

A full report on the OdLL Project can be found at www.opendoor2languages.net

2. Planning and practicalities

For the purposes of this handbook, open learning will be defined as learning that is flexible, self-directed and non-traditional (i.e. not classroom based). The community of learners, therefore, will largely be autonomous, non-specialists in language learning who, once engaged will need to be supported in a number of ways.

2.1 Why develop an open learning programme?

Key recommendations

a. Don't reinvent the wheel - use and adapt existing programmes, planning checklists, feedback and evaluation forms, etc. (see *Photocopiable materials*)
b. Build in systems for learner assessment, monitoring, and feedback (see *Assessment, Monitoring and Evaluation*)
c. Consider questions of costs (see *Funding*) and long term viability (see *Replicability and sustainability*)
d. Be aware that unforeseen problems will arise, so be flexible and remember that your programme is learner-centred

? Why am I doing this?

This is both an obvious and easily overlooked question that needs to be addressed from the outset. The programmes and models that are outlined in this handbook are predominantly learner-centred, thus the planning process should begin with a clear idea of what you hope your learners will be able to achieve by participating in your programme. Not only will a well defined set of aims and objectives facilitate the planning and the evaluation process, but it will also be useful for learner recruitment and publicity. There may also be benefits for yourself, your organisation, and the partners with whom you are working and these must also be considered early on in the planning process. These might include improving the profile of your organisation, reaching a new set of learners, and promoting language learning to the local community. This is of particular importance if you need to seek funding or cooperation from either within or outside your organisation.

2.2 Assessing learner needs and goals

Key recommendations

a. The earlier you find out what learners want, the better
b. Rely mainly on a written questionnaire to collect your data
c. Make the questionnaire as convenient for the learner as possible by using mostly closed question types but give the learner a chance to add extra information with at least one open question
d. Be flexible and able to adapt to learner needs

Introduction

Learner needs and goals should be assessed before you begin your programme. That way, you can design the programme to meet their needs. Or, if your programme is already designed, you can either adapt it or select learners whose goals are compatible with it.

What do learners want or need?

Learners may benefit from:
- New ways of learning
- Access to new or different materials
- Acquiring new skills
- Support from language experts
- A relaxed and informal learning environment
- Confidence-building activities
- Being encouraged to become more self-aware and reflective learners
- Being motivated
- Making new friends
- Having access to conversation practice
- Gaining a certificate or other credits for their learning
- Having a structure within which to learn (outside the classroom)

 How do I find out what my learners' needs are?

You can discuss their needs with them or, better still, give learners a questionnaire (*see Photocopiable materials: Learner profile form*). This will provide you with a more permanent record of their needs and goals. Make it user-friendly by giving them boxes to tick rather than full sentences to write - this will also be easier for you to analyse later. However, remember that no list of closed questions can ever be comprehensive, so include at least one open question to capture information that would otherwise not be recorded. The best time to find out about your learners' needs is during the planning or application process.

 What exactly will I ask my learners?

Find out what the learners intend to do with the language. Do they want mainly to read and write the language, or do they intend to focus on listening or speaking? Will they be using the language for leisure or work purposes? It is also useful for them to reflect on their previous language learning experiences (what worked or otherwise) and to perform, where relevant, a simple self-assessment (*see Photocopiable materials: Learner self-assessment form*).

 What will I do with the information I obtain?

If you identify learner needs before you design your programme, you can use the learner preferences to shape the content and the approach you take. For example, if a majority of learners want to be able to watch television and listen to the radio in the target language and very few want to use the language in letters or emails, then it would make sense to focus more on aural skills and encourage the use of audio-visual equipment.

If your programme is already designed, you could use the questionnaire data to select learners whose goals are more likely to be met by your programme or make amendments to it to meet these needs. If needs are very variable, you will have to try to make your programme as open and flexible as possible.

Discuss your learners' goals with them and encourage them to reflect upon how realistic these goals are in the short and long term. Learners will easily become discouraged if they have set themselves unrealistic goals. The tendency to see fluency as the only or main goal for language learning can be a major demotivator for language learners who may become discouraged because they have neither the time nor the opportunity to reach it. Many learners have ambitions for using the language which do not depend on fluency and they can be encouraged to set goals accordingly.

Case study 1

Supporting language learners with special needs

Distance learning for non-traditional language learners was a three-month language course for deaf and hard-of-hearing learners offering German and English language courses at four levels. It aimed to raise the learners' interest in language learning and provide them with a range of language learning strategies. It also offered guidelines on how to become independent, autonomous language learners.

The programme was set up and run by Cambridge University Press (Hungary) in collaboration with the British Council Hungary, Max Hueber Publishing House, the Goethe-Institut and the National Association for the Deaf and Hard of Hearing.

The programme recruited participants by sending out course information leaflets with the help of the partners listed above. Once applications had been collected and learners selected, a timetable was drawn up and course arrangements were made - setting up groups by using placement tests, distributing course books and booking venues. Materials were selected and prepared based on participants' needs. During the learning phase instructions were sent out to learners referring to materials in the course books, work was collected and corrected (via email) on a regular basis and face-to-face consultation sessions were run to give some additional support.

This method of language learning seemed to be the preferred way for deaf and hard-of-hearing learners. Face-to-face sessions provided learning and language advice as well as offering speaking and lip-reading practice. Otherwise developing reading and writing skills was the main focus. At the end of the programme learners were asked to give their responses:

> "I have learnt to be **more autonomous**"
> "I liked the project because I could learn at **my own pace at home**"
> "I liked it as this was **something new and unusual** and I like this **method**"
> "I liked the **independence** and the fact that we had **to motivate ourselves**"

The programme booklet and the information on the website made it reasonably easy to run the courses, however in terms of the learners' special needs course books specially designed for the deaf and hard-of-hearing would definitely have helped to increase their chances of success.

2.3 Selecting a model

Key recommendations
a. Design a programme that combines three key elements: learner training; access to learning materials; and access to a support network of fellow learners, teachers or native speakers
b. Be aware of existing local provision for language learning

Introduction
During the two trial phases of the OdLL Project, a total of fourteen tests were conducted. These have been categorised into six open learning model types (*See Table 1: Open learning models*). Further information about each test is available on the OdLL Project website: www.opendoor2languages.net and in the nine case studies presented in this publication.

 What will I offer?

What you offer will depend upon your particular expertise, the needs of your learners and the aims and objectives you have subsequently identified. For example, if you decide that one of the main aims of your programme is to progressively develop learner autonomy, you may choose to adopt a learner training programme. If, on the other hand, you are planning a one-off event to develop language or cultural awareness, a roadshow or taster day will be a more appropriate option.

There are advantages and disadvantages to all the open learning models tested. For example, while a distance learning model allows learners to work at their own pace, the lack of speaking opportunities can be a problem. The negative aspects of a particular model can be lessened or eradicated by combining elements from various models. None of the models tested are mutually exclusive and the most successful programmes combine elements of learner training, access to learning materials and a support network of fellow learners, teachers and native speakers.

When selecting a model it is also important to take account of local conditions, e.g.:
•   The types of non-traditional learning available
•   Attitudes to independent versus traditional language learning
•   Access to learning materials and support tools
•   Opportunities for cooperation

2.4 Funding

Key recommendations
a. Ask your learners to pay a fee (free is not always interpreted as good)
b. Work with other organisations to help spread the cost

Introduction
The European Community funded the OdLL Project so language learning programmes were offered at no cost to the learners. However, in order to replicate the models funding is a vital consideration which will need to be considered early on in the planning process. It is easy to underestimate the amount of time and staff costs involved in planning, running and evaluating an open learning programme. However, there are a number of ways of recovering costs.

 ## What costs are involved?

Costs vary from programme to programme and will be influenced by what you can incorporate into your normal activities and what you need to make special provision for. Costs include:

- Staff
- Facilities (e.g. room hire)
- Publicity
- Learning materials (purchase or development)
- Technology (e.g. hardware or software purchase or web development)

One of the first things you need to consider when drafting a budget is the duration of the programme (*see Setting a timetable*). You can then estimate the budget, taking into account the different phases into which the programme will be divided. Once the budget is drafted in detail, you may need to look for additional sources of funding, e.g. grants, subsidies or learner fees.

 ## Will it only be my organisation that pays these costs?

Not necessarily. There are many ways to get extra financial support for your programme. You may think of working with other similar organisations (both public and private), of establishing cooperative networks, or of contacting organisations at a local or national level, e.g. the Education Authority. Such organisations may be able to provide support, give a higher profile to the programme and advise on possible national funds available. Partners' contributions may be in kind rather than via direct financial subsidies, e.g. the British Council and the Goethe-Institut helped by donating materials and providing venues for the OdLL Project. Another possibility is to submit a funding proposal to the European Community.

 ## Are there ways of limiting costs?

Possibly the best way to limit costs is to rely on your own organisation's staff to devise and manage the whole programme. Subcontracting may be an option but only for specific tasks, which may require a different professional profile. Learning materials, publicity, and dissemination can be expensive, so try to make use of what is already available. It is always a good idea to look for cooperation with organisations with complementary specialisms, such as publishers or publicity agencies that can cover some costs if they act as sponsors.

 ## How will I integrate this programme into the normal activities of my organisation?

The first step is to promote the project to all staff. If the programme is fully supported by your senior management, it will be easier to develop. Indeed, this support can be essential for a successful programme, particularly where staff time and funding from within your organisation are required.

 ## Will I expect learners to pay and if so what for and how much?

Unless you have special funding, learners will normally be expected to pay for participating in programmes that require the regular presence of a language teacher or the provision of learning materials. Indeed, the payment of a fee by learners, even a modest one, can prove to be a motivating force. You need to consider the real costs to you and decide whether your learners would be prepared to pay these costs in full or whether you will have to obtain a subsidy from elsewhere.

2.5 Publicity and recruitment

Key recommendations
a. Allow plenty of time to recruit learners
b. Don't rely solely on leaflets and posters
c. Use advertisements in local newspapers where possible. A tight budget need not be a limitation as some publications allow you to advertise for free.
d. Ensure that your publicity is clear about exactly what is on offer, what learning outcomes are expected and who is eligible to participate

Introduction
If you want to run an open learning programme, you will, of course, need learners. This section offers advice on how to publicise your programme and recruit learners.

 Do I have a budget to spend on recruiting?

Having funds available to target learners enables you to take out paid advertisements in newspapers or on local radio. The OdLL Project found that advertisements in local newspapers attracted large numbers of potential learners. However, press advertisements can be expensive so if funds for publicity are limited you may consider alternatives such as issuing a press release through your organisation.

 How will I disseminate information?

There are many ways to publicise activities and recruit learners. These might include the following:
- Free and paid advertisements in local newspapers
- Posters, leaflets and bookmarks
- Advertisments on your own or your partner institution's website
- Meetings with potentially interested parties
- In-house newspapers, bulletins, networks (for internal publicity)
- Public Relations departments
- Direct written contact with interested parties
- Contact with former learners
- Contact with local organisations, e.g. local government
- National organisations and government departments
- Radio advertisements

During the OdLL Project newspaper advertisements produced very good results but leaflets and posters were less effective.

 What type of learners will I target?

You may decide to target learners with a specific set of circumstances or needs (e.g. parents, hearing-impaired, people who work together), or you may aim at a wider public. You may also decide that learners need particular qualifications or past experiences of language learning.

❓ How many learners do I want to reach? How many can I afford to accommodate?

Remember that for every learner taking part in your programme, there will be associated administrative work. This could include selection, monitoring, advising, testing, and feedback gathering. Also, greater numbers of learners place more strain on the resources available - both learning materials and staff. Numbers must be large enough for the programme to be cost-effective but small enough to encourage a group dynamic and facilitate effective learning. Large groups may be sub-divided for particular activities. In certain circumstances mixed ability groups, and even mixed language groups work very well, e.g. on a learner training programme or language roadshow.

❓ Have I described the programme clearly enough in my promotional materials?

If you are looking for learners of a certain profile, e.g. beginners only, make sure you state this clearly in your advertising. This will prevent applicants from forming false expectations and will save you time later. If your programme requires certain skills (e.g. elementary computing) or the use of certain equipment (e.g. video, mobile telephones) be sure to mention this in your promotional literature so that you won't have to disappoint ineligible applicants later on.

❓ Do I intend to select learners or will I accept all applicants?

Regardless of how accurately you describe your model, you may still get applicants who are not suitable for your programme. Placement tests, tasks and interviews can be used to select learners, but make sure you have the resources to cope with the additional workload that selecting entails. If your programme depends upon learners having particular skills, make this clear or try to test this from the outset. For example, one way of ensuring that learners are computer literate is to make the application process email based. If you are going to be selective or if places are limited, then say so in your promotional literature. Use a learner profile form (see *Photocopiable materials: Learner profile form*) to collect socio-economic data and to help with the selection process.

❓ Are there good and bad times to recruit?

Generally summer is not a particularly good time to advertise or run courses because people tend to take holidays and pursue more outdoor activities.

2.6 Languages

❓ What language(s) will I offer?

Ideally, an open learning programme will offer learners a free choice of languages and encourage the take-up of less widely used, less taught languages, but in reality the availability of learning materials, expertise and learner demand will limit the languages on offer. You may decide to offer just one language, several languages of your or the learners' choice, or give learners a free choice.

2.7 Setting a timetable

Key recommendations

a. Consider the profile of your learners (age, employment status, geographical situation, etc.) when selecting the timing for your activities
b. Don't run your programme during the summer vacation period

Introduction

For adults balancing their learning with other activities in their lives, issues of time are a key concern and can act as a major barrier to success. The time of day, frequency of meetings and classes as well as opening times of language resource centres will all have a major impact. However, as one OdLL learner comments: "We all have the same amount of time, it is how we apportion it."

 **How much time do I have available to organise and run my programme?**

Having a sense of how much time both organisers and other staff will have to devote to the project will play a key part in the development of your programme, determining such factors as how many sessions you run, how much development of new materials is possible and what type of assessment will be included. It is essential to be realistic when estimating the amount of time each person involved in delivering the programme can devote to it, taking account of preparation, marking, contact hours with learners, etc.

How much time will learners be expected to spend on their learning (daily, weekly, over the whole programme)?

Consider the target group when deciding upon the time that learners will be expected to spend on their language learning. For example, unemployed and retired people will be able to devote more time than those in full-time employment.

What day of the week and time will the sessions be? Will they be on the same or different day and time each week or fortnight?

Whatever the length of the programme, it is advisable to establish a regular attendance calendar for the learning sessions (face-to-face, self-study or online). Your learners will probably need help in setting and maintaining a realistic schedule for self-study, as time management is a skill in itself. Also, the time of the year that you run your programme is important, e.g. if you try to run a programme over the summer it may be difficult to find staff, and learners may lose motivation if they have a break in their studies due to a vacation.

How long will my programme last? How many activities will there be? Will I organise the activities weekly, every two weeks...?

The duration and number of activities in your programme will need to be adapted to the target group, and should be flexible enough to adapt to learners' demands. Contact sessions should probably not be more than one or two weeks apart in order to maintain continuity. Feedback from the OdLL Project showed that having a very short course suited learners who found the commitment of a longer programme too restricting, while others preferred to have meetings spread over a longer period (e.g. at two-weekly rather than weekly intervals).

 Will there be any compulsion for learners to attend some or all sessions?

A certain degree of compulsion is frequently desirable for both teacher and learner. By insisting that learners attend the first session, you can ensure that they receive a proper introduction to the programme, and compulsory attendance at the final session will help you gather feedback. You may consider offering a reward of some kind or an attendance certificate as an incentive.

2.8 Selecting a venue

Key recommendations
a. Identify which type of facilities your model will require. If possible, try organising the programme using your own facilities; if not, look for alternative solutions.
b. Be prepared to pay a fee to use external facilities and book well in advance
c. Try to give your learners access to a resource centre but be aware that they may prefer or need to work at home

Introduction
You may have all the facilities you need within your own organisation but if not it might be necessary to use external venues and facilities.

 What kind of facilities do I have and are these appropriate to my programme?

In some cases, the facilities you have in your organisation will be adequate. For example, if you run a distance learning model, you will not have specific location requirements. However, if you wish, for example, to run a roadshow or a taster day, or if you want to use films, music or other activities in your programme, you will need to consider where you will hold these sessions. In addition, if you are opening access to technology and learning materials, a regular classroom might not be sufficient. In these cases, you may want to look for facilities outside of your organisation. Even in cases where you have the required facilities within your own organisation, you may consider using a less formal venue or one with better access times. Some learners may find the prospect of using a language resource centre based in a university or college intimidating and would be happier in more familiar surroundings such as a library or community centre.

 Are there other facilities that I could use outside my organisation?

In cases where your own organisation's facilities are not sufficient, you might think of working with other organisations. Suitable venues include:
• Community centres (these may include rooms in places of worship)
• Internet centres
• Cafés and restaurants
• Libraries
• Classrooms (in schools or colleges)
• Public language resource centres

 How can I make the venue attractive?

Access is a major consideration in terms of distance, opening times, and learning materials. In order to create an atmosphere which makes the learning process a pleasant activity, it may be necessary to adapt a rented classroom in an educational organisation or a room in a youth centre or library, e.g. by bringing in audio-visual equipment, a computer or learning materials; moving furniture; putting up posters, etc.

Will external facilities be free or will there be a hire charge?

In some cases, other organisations will be very cooperative and willing to make their facilities available for free, as it is an opportunity for them to attract new customers or users. In other cases they will take more convincing that they should allow you to use their facilities and you may also have to pay a fee. However, you may be able to negotiate the price if you are providing a public service. Public libraries may make their facilities available for free but may appreciate new materials in return. Think about booking well in advance, especially in the case of public centres.

 How much learning will be done in the learner's own home?

The amount of work that will be done by your learners outside of meeting times depends on the degree of learner independence in your programme. Even for programmes with a lower level of independence, it is advisable to provide your learners with some extra tasks or to suggest additional learning materials (e.g. those freely available on the Internet) in order to stimulate motivation and interest. However, you cannot expect your learners to have all necessary technology and learning materials in their homes. Therefore, you might think about extending the opening hours of your language resource centre although this has implications for staffing and possibly security. In some cases, there may be copyright issues in allowing learners, who are not registered students, access to your facilities and learning materials. One solution may be to make them members of your resource centre for the duration of the programme.

Case study 2

Language roadshow

The *Language roadshow* was a ten-day event designed to bring a wider variety of language materials to learners in remote areas. It was designed for secondary school students, their teachers and parents and aimed to demonstrate self-study materials, introduce independent learning techniques and provide information about language learning opportunities in the local area.

The roadshow included 45-minute interactive presentations using video, audiocassettes, CD-ROMs and the Internet. The video and audiocassette based materials were accompanied by worksheets to be completed independently by the students.

The roadshow was run by Cambridge University Press (Hungary) in collaboration with the British Council Hungary and its Resource Centres, Klett Publishing House, the Goethe-Institut, Vár Language School (Kisvárda), ILS Language School and Bookshop (Nyíregyháza) and Libra Bookshop (Budapest). Twelve secondary, grammar and vocational schools in nine small towns and villages were involved.

Cambridge University Press and its partners provided learning materials to be shown and given to participants. These materials included books, readers, dictionaries, video and audiocassettes, CD-ROMs and a list of useful websites. This method of learner training was popular with young learners as it showed them different and non-traditional ways of learning, e.g. alternatives to using a textbook. This meant that take-up was very high with only one school pulling out due to timetabling problems.

The sessions were lively and the students welcomed the varied activities, as did their teachers who appreciated the materials, ideas and techniques provided. Teachers were also helpful in organising the sessions and grouping students based on language levels.

2.9 Staff

Key recommendations

a. Determine whether you are able to employ all required staff before you start the programme
b. Use staff with a variety of competences
c. Try to use native speakers and language students in your programme, where appropriate

Introduction

Staffing is one of the most important elements of your programme. You may decide to work with staff from inside or outside your own organisation. Depending on which model you have chosen, you will need different people who are able to cope with the various aspects of the programme. These may include:

- Coordinators overseeing the programme (including project managers, directors and secretaries)
- Facilitators and coaches
- Teachers
- Native speakers
- Learning advisors
- Web developers
- Technicians
- Materials designers
- Library staff

❓ How many members of staff do I need?

The number of staff you will need depends on the model that you have chosen as a basis for your programme. Some model types require several staff with different skills, e.g. distance e-learning. Other types will require only a small number of staff, e.g. open access or study groups. It is best to identify your needs in terms of staff before you start recruiting learners for your programme.

❓ What kind of staff do I need and what roles will they have?

The type of programme you are offering will, of course, dictate the type of staff you will need. In some cases your staff will have to be technically skilled, in others their competence will have to be pedagogic. For example, a distance e-learning model where you are offering online exercises will need someone who is able to load materials onto the website, but will also need a teacher to select or write them. You may also want to use native speakers as they are very popular with learners and provide an authentic conversation experience. Bear in mind that in a non-traditional and open learning programme the role of the teacher may differ somewhat from that of a traditional classroom instructor (see *Learner support*). Finally, you may wish to have someone who can monitor the entire programme, checking on attendance and keeping in contact with learners.

❓ How many staff hours will I need and can I afford?

You should take into account that the organisation of a programme could involve a considerable amount of work. Preparation and recruitment are time-consuming, and in some cases, staff will be working on the programme in addition to their normal working hours. Therefore, it is useful to make a realistic estimate of the staff hours and the cost of this. The cheapest option is to try to incorporate the programme and its organisation into the normal, existing hours of your staff. However, that will sometimes be impossible, so you may have to ask your staff to work overtime or employ someone new. What you can afford will depend on why you are developing the programme (e.g. to perform a public service or to sell courses). You may have acquired or wish to seek special funding (see *Funding*). The most sensible solution is to check with your management and your financial department to see what is affordable.

Will I be able to use students in my programme and what is in it for them?

Where possible, try to involve student volunteers in your programme: they are obviously cost-effective, and since they are volunteers, they will usually be very motivated. Bear in mind, however, that they may be inexperienced and will need support and supervision. Being involved in an open learning programme is a great experience for students, especially if they want to become teachers themselves.

If you have the means to reward them for their contribution, you could give them a book token or CD voucher. You could also pay them as a staff member, but that will be more expensive and also more complicated. If you include a tandem-learning element (i.e. a system in which two learners of different languages exchange conversation) in your programme this may be sufficient reward for the student. More information on tandem learning can be found at: www.enst.fr/tandem/etandem/etindex-en.html

 Will I need to train my staff?

If you plan to use teaching staff (e.g. native speakers) who have no prior teaching experience, then they will need training and support. Experienced teachers may also need to be given some induction into your programme, especially if it involves a non-traditional or new way of learning.

 How will I train my staff?

You may need to run one or more face-to-face training sessions or consultations or you may write some guidance notes for your teachers. This will also help to make your programme reusable (*see Replicability and sustainability*).

2.10 Cooperation with others

Key recommendations
a. Find partners with skills, expertise and facilities to complement your own and offer them something in return
b. Don't work with too many partners
c. Liaise with a particular person rather than an organisation and keep in regular contact
d. Set clear goals and an exact timetable to avoid misunderstandings

Introduction
This section offers advice on how to identify, contact and work with partners. It also highlights some of the benefits and shortcomings of this type of cooperation.

 How do I identify and contact partners?

The nature of your programme and the needs of your learners may guide you towards several prospective partners. You may contact people with whom you have cooperated in the past, or people whose interests, capability and reliability you know about. You may also choose a partner who has complementary skills and facilities to your own.

www.opendoor2languages.net

 Who will I be working with? Staff from outside or inside my own organisation?

It is easier to establish partnerships in places where there are existing networks but it is well worth making the effort to develop relationships with new partners. Moreover, it is advisable to contact named individuals within an organisation. Look for willing partners who are committed to working with you towards success and who are not just interested in financial gain.

 What benefits will the prospective partner receive?

It will help if you can demonstrate what benefits the prospective partner will receive from cooperation, e.g. help with disseminating their materials and increasing their audience (more library users, more people buying books or enrolling for formal classes, recruiting more learners).

 What form will the cooperation take?

Cooperation may take various forms:
- Running the same model in a different location or region or at a different time
- Providing a venue
- Development or provision of learning materials
- Technological support
- Consultancy and advice

 How will the partnership be managed?

If you are drawing up a formal partnership you may wish to set up a contract of agreement (see below). Otherwise it is advisable to be clear about the role your partner(s) will have and how and to whom staff will be reporting. Having regular meetings (face-to-face or virtual) will help to check on progress, deal with problems and evaluate the programme.

 Will I need to draw up formal contracts or letters of agreement?

Formal agreements define responsibilities and give protection to both sides. Setting clear guidelines on project expenses will reduce the possibility of later misunderstandings and will also help if you are making a financial agreement with your partners. It is also advisable to draw up a timetable of the main activities and agree it with the staff concerned.

Some possible benefits of cooperation:
- Access to complementary skills
- Breaking down barriers between sectors (public and private or schools, colleges and universities)
- Sharing expertise and ideas
- Access to more or different materials

Some possible shortcomings of cooperation:
- Bureaucratic obstacles (form filling, approval by committee, etc.)
- Partners withdrawing from the programme at the last minute (a formal contract may prevent this problem)
- Lack of awareness and cooperation between departments within the same organisation (could also be a benefit if cooperation resolves this)
- Competition between organisations

Copyright © 2005 OdLL Project partners. May be copied provided source is acknowledged.

Case study 3

Working with public centres

This project set up a language resource centre (LRC) in Zaragoza Public Library for children aged 6-14. The purpose of the project was to motivate the very young to learn languages and to widen access to language learning materials. It also explored the possibilities for cooperation between a private company devoted to education and training (mt Educación y Formación) and a publicly funded organisation.

The project offered two types of access to language learning. The first of these consisted of open access to the public on Monday-Friday afternoons and Saturday mornings. Users had access to a language learning advisor and could participate in language learning activities. These included writing about their own language, country and culture; adding to the Babel Tower (a display of words in languages other than Spanish); finding out about the different languages spoken in the city via the *Languagemeter*; and discussing their language learning strategies via a noticeboard.

The second type of learning consisted of guided visits for schools, which took place once a week in the mornings. A group of fifty pupils was divided into two subgroups according to age. They were given an introduction to the LRC and the available materials, and participated in language learning activities, e.g. storytelling.

To support the activities and use of the LRC visitors had access to written materials (e.g. books, stories, songs), audio-visual materials (e.g. DVD, videos, CDs), and language advisors, who guided the activities and advised learners on the best use of materials.

The success of this project was due to several different factors: the methodology; a selection of very attractive materials which captured the imagination of the users; the activities with the children (especially story-telling); the support of a language advisor as opposed to a teacher; and the high degree of attendance and positive response from children, parents and teachers. This is illustrated by the following feedback comments:

"I consider it to be a very **enriching and encouraging experience**. I can learn a language at the same time as playing with other children."

"The language advisors have been very **kind and professional with the children**, and the activities planned in the LRC were very entertaining"

"It is an **innovative** method to teach children a language in **an enjoyable and playful way**"

"The display of activities on boards was warmly welcomed. Children were eager to participate. Everybody could see it! **They were teaching everybody**!"

The main challenge was gaining the trust and cooperation of the public library as this was a new experience for them and they were understandably wary at first. However after a series of discussions with the Library Director and his team, a very successful working relationship was established. The following are comments made by the Library Director:

"This is a **useful and interesting experience** that allows us to focus people's attention on language resources, by giving prominence to these materials"

"This pilot experience has been a **very important initiative** because it has shown children and youngsters what they can do in their local library while they are learning languages"

3. Pedagogic issues

3.1 Learner support

Key recommendations

a. Be aware of the multiple roles that a teacher can adopt, e.g. facilitator, counsellor or resource
b. Start with a learner needs analysis (see *Assessing learner needs and goals*)
c. Bear in mind what the learners want and can do
d. Keep in contact with learners

Introduction

For a programme that has a strong element of both learner autonomy and flexibility, systems of learner support are a vital component. Such support may take the form of a structured training programme or it may be on a more ad-hoc basis, such as providing access to a website or the email address of a language advisor. It may also be face-to-face, or via a pack of printed materials supplied at the beginning of the programme. Indeed any combination of these may apply.

❓ What is the role of the teacher?

Some of the potential roles a teacher may adopt are detailed below (Ideas taken from Voller, P. (1997) 'Does the teacher have a role in autonomous learning?' In P. Benson and P. Voller (eds) *Autonomy and Independence in Language Learning*. London: Longman.):

As a **facilitator** the teacher ensures that the appropriate conditions and environment for learning are in place. This can be achieved by:
*   Helping learners to identify their needs, goals, strengths and weaknesses
    (see *Assessing learner needs and goals*)
*   Providing learning models which match the needs of an individual learner or group of learners
    (see *Table 1: Open learning models*)
*   Creating a positive learning environment
*   Taking account of specific needs and learning styles
*   Fostering self-monitoring and record-keeping (see *Monitoring*)
*   Considering and offering appropriate assessment tools (see *Assessment*)
*   Stimulating cooperative learning

In the role of **counsellor** a teacher might be responsible for motivating learners, raising their awareness of the benefits of autonomous learning and boosting their self-esteem. Good communication between the teacher and the learner is of great importance here. This communication may take place in the following ways:
*   Class or group activities
*   Face-to-face communication in the classroom, tutorials and other feedback sessions
*   Meetings and advice sessions
*   Telephone or video conferencing
*   Discussion groups - face-to-face or virtual
*   Email, discussion lists, chat rooms
*   Feedback forms

Finally the teacher will also act as a **resource** providing both subject expertise and general learning advice. This may include:

- How to improve linguistic skills
- How to identify and use learning strategies
- The retrieval of information from the wide range of learning materials available
- The development of key skills, such as technical skills (e.g. web browsing, email, word processing, etc.)

Having identified such a variety of different roles for the teacher it must be emphasised that this need not imply that all of these roles are independent of each other (a teacher may act as a resource and counsellor at the same time) or that they will all be carried out by just one person.

 What learning support should be available to learners and what form will this take?

In places where independent or non-traditional language learning is a relatively new concept, learners will need greater levels of support in order to adapt to different ways of learning. Even if you are running a programme which involves a high level of learner autonomy from the start, it is advisable to hold at least one induction session so that learners are clear about where to find learning materials, how they can get help, etc. While learners often require a higher level of support, particularly in the early stages, it is important to encourage autonomy and to guard against over-dependency on the teacher or facilitator.

Some ideas to consider:

- Be available but not too available, i.e. specify times when you can be contacted
- Computer and technical assistance could be useful
- A list of language learning techniques should be provided to facilitate independent learning, either in a learning pack or presented in face-to-face sessions
- Find a venue within easy reach for face-to-face sessions
- The timetable for face-to-face sessions should take account of the participants' other commitments, e.g. not necessarily within normal working hours
- Make further learning materials and opportunities for developing skills available

 Will teachers be in face-to-face or virtual contact with students?

For certain types of open learning programmes, such as taster days, language advising and study groups, face-to-face sessions are vital. In other types, they will add value to your programme, but may not necessarily be affordable. Alternatively, you might think of using virtual contact. This could be a good solution where learners are at a considerable distance from the learning centre or in other cases where it is difficult to bring all your students together in one place. Telephone conferencing is a simple, relatively cheap solution while video conferencing is a very effective but more expensive option. You might also think about using the Internet for maintaining contact: email, web forums and chat rooms are an excellent and cheap way to keep in touch. Using mobile telephones for SMS text-messaging is another simple option.

Case study 4

Language advice service for parents

The *Language advice service* was run for parents in Zaragoza whose children were in secondary education learning English, and who wanted to be able to help with their language learning. It had two main elements: virtual contact and face-to-face sessions. For the first of these there was a website where parents could find materials (tips, activities, grammar, links) to help them learn or refresh their language knowledge. They could also receive language advice via email, and they could give their opinions on language learning and meet people with similar interests in the forum. For the second element five sessions were offered. These dealt with general tips on motivation; grammar help; activities to help develop vocabulary; and techniques for improving language skills (reading, writing, speaking and listening). In the sessions parents were invited to ask questions relating to their own language competence as well as being given suggestions for materials and techniques that they could use when working with their children.

To support the face-to-face sessions, participants were given a series of written materials and access to a website from which other materials could be downloaded.

The most successful aspects of this project were that the online language advice service was complemented by the face-to-face sessions, it encouraged participants to practise weekly tips at home and it was very practical.

Feedback from participants indicated that approaching language learning in this way was very innovative and interesting:

> "It is very difficult to find **language learning tips** that are aimed at parents"

> "I decided to take part in this experience because it seemed different. However, I think it should be longer. **I wish it could continue**."

Case study 5

Creating social conditions for language learning

The *Spanish conversation club* was a programme that was almost entirely focussed on conversation and which took place in an informal and sociable atmosphere. It aimed to increase confidence in oral skills, stimulate independence, give access to native speakers and provide an opportunity to meet with fellow learners.

The programme included six conversation sessions, three film evenings, and two informal dinners. It was designed and run by Lessius Hogeschool (Antwerp, Belgium), and for the film activities there was cooperation with a local community centre.

All conversation sessions took place at Lessius Hogeschool. There were twenty participants in the group, but this was subdivided into smaller groups so people felt more confident about speaking. Each group was guided by a coach, who was a Spanish exchange student.

The sessions were organised every fortnight and lasted two hours each. During the sessions, participants talked about themselves, their interests, and their favourite Spanish-speaking region. Later on, face-to-face interviews, role-plays, listening exercises, and a quiz were used. Learners also talked about their everyday lives, e.g. vacations, work, restaurant visits, ambitions and interests.

The conversation sessions were followed by three Spanish film screenings. These were preceded by an introduction and followed by a discussion about the film. Additionally, learners were invited to meet in a tapas bar, where they could talk informally in Spanish with each other and the coaches.

This approach turned out to be very popular with learners, especially as conversation-only classes are hard to find in Belgium.

The sessions were friendly and informal and although it was a very mixed group (age and level) the formula seemed to work well. Indeed, some learners began to contact each other outside of the group meetings. Many learners commented that they felt that they had gained in confidence and appreciated that the group was focussed on conversation and informal:

> "I liked the fact that **conversation was the main concern**, which is difficult to find in normal evening classes. This is usually too school-like: you have to use a handbook, there is very little time to be creative."

> "I liked the fact that all people in my group had a different level of speech... But thanks to the coaches we **all managed to talk** to one another!"

3.2 Motivation

Key recommendations
a. Be clear about what your programme is offering
b. Give support to learners (online or face-to-face) especially at the beginning
c. Introduce an incentive, e.g. charge a fee to be reimbursed at the end or offer a certificate

Introduction
In the Eurobarometer Special Survey (2001)* one of the identified barriers to language learning was lack of motivation. This section looks at motivation as an important factor in learner achievement.

* http://europa.eu.int/comm/public_opinion/archives/ebs/ebs_147_summ_en.pdf

How can I motivate non-traditional learners to start studying languages in an open learning programme?

Firstly, ask your learners about their goals and personal motivations for learning a language (*see Assessing learner needs and goals*). It is easier to motivate people to start studying independently if the product suits their needs.

Here are some suggestions for attracting non-traditional learners' interest:
- Offer a programme which has flexibility: "What I liked was that I could learn English at home, undisturbed, at my own pace" (Learner, OdLL Project)
- Offer easy access to the classroom, library or resource centre
- Hold taster days where learners come and try things out
- Ask your learners what they want and design a programme to meet their needs and interests
- Offer something new (e.g. film club, drama, video)
- Help learners to identify their own motivational or learning style
- Offer activities at an appropriate language level (this may mean differentiated activities for a mixed ability group)
- Include some form of assessment or self-evaluation (*see Assessment*)

How can I maintain learners' motivation once I have got them started?

Even if motivation is high at the beginning, the problem is how to sustain it throughout the programme. Independence and flexibility demand a great deal of self-discipline. Support is very important at this stage, whether it is via face-to-face meetings or online assistance. However, consider the balance between independent working and guidance, i.e. how to provide adequate support without undermining individual initiative.

Here are some suggestions to keep learners motivated:
- Provide regular feedback and encouragement
- Encourage learners to complete a learner's log
- Recommend a course book or study guide
- Set tasks to hand in
- Provide a variety of learning materials (written or online) including authentic materials: "Games motivate - you think about them and try to repeat the challenge" (Learner, OdLL Project)
- Include a social element - hold informal meetings with or without the teacher, e.g. in a pub, café or restaurant
- Encourage learners to form study groups
- Provide opportunities for conversation
- Learning to learn - show learners how they can become autonomous language learners
- Use native speakers

 How can I encourage learners to reach their goals?

An important consideration for the success of this kind of programme is that learners' goals are set at the right level. Some learners will see fluency as the main goal, which may be unrealistic in terms of the time they have available for learning. Strategies on how to learn may help learners to be realistic about their goals. Another more traditional way of encouraging learners is to offer an examination, although this is not the case for all learners as some may be deterred by a formal test. You could also offer some sort of reward at the end of the programme, e.g. a book or book token, or ask learners to make a financial contribution, which could be reimbursed on completion of the programme.

Even if you believe that motivation should come from within, learners will still need your support. Here are some more suggestions:
- Set realistic and clear goals both for the learner and the teacher
- Let learners set their own goals: "I make my study plan for each week. And I plan to do the examination as soon as possible. It encourages me to reach my target." (Learner, OdLL Project)
- Help learners to become reflective and to make judgements on their progress
- Use different types of contact, e.g. face-to-face meetings, telephone, email, chat rooms, SMS text-messaging
- Hold regular meetings
- Provide a certificate of attendance for those who complete the course

www.opendoor2languages.net

Case study 6

Using drama to motivate learners

Drama was used with groups of learners at the National University of Ireland, Maynooth to develop their production (speaking) skills in Irish. Scripting and presenting short plays or dialogues is also a way to develop writing skills (during the scripting stage), and listening skills (during rehearsal and performance). Writing drama gets learners involved because they have a chance to be creative. And because they are performing their own work, learners are motivated to do well. A key aim of the dramas was to help develop oral and aural skills, but also to encourage learner contact off-campus using an activity that required learners to work together.

In two groups facilitators introduced the idea of a drama, oversaw the creation of teams (three or four learners in each), discussed situations and characters, and set production deadlines. In one group, plays were to be performed the following week; in the other, learners were given a fortnight to prepare. As learners devised ideas, they checked grammar and vocabulary with the teachers.

After the initial session, learners worked on the script at home, both on their own and in partnership with other team members via telephone and email. In the performance session, teams were given an opportunity to rehearse and make final changes to their script before going on stage.

Performances lasted between five and fifteen minutes. One performance was filmed.

Feedback was collected from two different sources - a drama activity evaluation form completed immediately after the performances and the standard exit feedback form (for the whole programme) completed some weeks later. Both of these indicated that the activity was well received.

The questions about preparing from home in partnership with others elicited a number of comments, both favourable and unfavourable. One learner found the preparation very useful because she "learned how to email", but not enjoyable because "the baby was on my lap while I was trying to compose [emails]." A number of learners reported difficulties in adjusting to other people's schedules and one learner found her preparation "unsuccessful due to the computer being unavailable all the time." Asked whether they would like to do an exercise of this type again all respondents answered "Yes."

In the exit feedback drama was the most popular activity, being mentioned by 44% as the most interesting or useful aspect of the programme. Comments included:

> "Drama was the best part of the course for me and **I learned a lot** of Irish from this exercise"

> "I **enjoyed devising the drama** with classmates"

> "It was a **very enjoyable and useful** means of using the language"

According to one of the facilitators, the learners "took ownership [of the play] and it allowed them to express themselves creatively in the target language." It also "helped to forge them into a proper group."

This activity could easily be replicated in other language learning programmes. In the face of severe difficulties for learners in allocating time at home and coordinating their schedules, the activity could be based entirely in the classroom. However, the lack of learner participation outside contact hours would have to be tackled by other means.

3.3 Assessment

Key recommendations:
a. Don't assess for its own sake (take account of what learners need or want)
b. Develop assessment to fit the programme offered
c. Have clear learning outcomes (organiser or learner defined) to guide your choice of assessment

Introduction
Below are some tools and methods that you might choose for your learning programme. However, before making your choice it is advisable to review the aims and objectives of your programme, the type of learners you are targetting and the type of learning you are supporting. Sometimes learners do not want to undertake formal assessment. For each participant, organiser and programme the value and purpose of assessment will vary, thus there are some key questions to consider from the outset.

 What to assess?

Some types of assessment are more focussed on the process of learning while others, such as tests and examinations are product-oriented. Thus deciding what you are assessing will help to determine whether to take a process or product approach. Here are some examples:
- Language skills - writing, reading, speaking (production), speaking (interaction), listening. PRODUCT
- Language learning skills - awareness and use of learning strategies, use of materials. PROCESS
- Key transferable skills - communication (literacy, oral, IT skills), working with others, problem-solving
- Learner independence - ability to set and achieve goals, self-directed learning, time management. PROCESS
- Affective factors - confidence, motivation, enjoyment

 Who or what is doing the assessment?

This will relate to how formal the assessment will be for your programme and will vary depending on whether it has a formative (e.g. feedback) or summative (e.g. examination) purpose. The assessor may be:
- The teacher or facilitator
- The learner
- The native speaker
- Other learners
- Computer
- Examiner

 How will I assess?

Some of the options for assessment are:
- Examination
- Presentation (e.g. giving talks, performing mini-dramas, making a video)
- Coursework (e.g. projects, essays, translations)
- Exercises (e.g. grammar, comprehension, multiple-choice)
- Diagnostic tests
- Portfolio (e.g. European Language Portfolio, learning journal or diary)
- Group work (e.g. role-play, cooperative projects)
- Participation in conversation (e.g. number of contributions to conversations, oral discussions or online discussions)

? **What is the expected outcome?**

Outcomes will be affected by the methods of assessment chosen but it is important that learners are given a clear idea of what they can expect to gain, e.g.:

- Externally validated certificate
- Internally validated certificate
- Grades or marks
- Corrections or comments
- Oral feedback
- Written feedback
- Level on the Common European Framework*
- Progression to the next level
- Desire to continue learning
- Personal satisfaction

*The Common European Framework of Reference for Languages is a Council of Europe initiative, which seeks to provide a means of assessing and reporting language competence that is recognised across the European Community. Further details can be found at:
www.coe.int/T/E/Cultural_Co-operation/education/Languages/Language_Policy/Common_Framework_of_Reference/default.asp

3.4 Monitoring

Key recommendations
a. Incorporate systems for maintaining records of learning and attendance
b. Ensure that communication is maintained with learners especially when they are working independently
c. Record learner profiles and collect feedback on the programme

Introduction
Giving weekly tasks, running regular (compulsory) meetings and keeping records of attendance not only enable you to monitor how the programme and your learners are progressing but they also serve as a powerful motivating force and will contribute greatly to your final evaluation of the programme.

"The weekly sessions keep you motivated, if you don't do the homework you get found out … Because I have no willpower that weekly goal to sort of give you a prod was very useful" (Learner, OdLL Project)

How will I monitor my programme?

Below are some suggestions for the types of and purposes for monitoring:

Type	Description	Purpose
Weekly tasks or homework	• Language tasks based either on a particular learning material, e.g. exercise or page from a book, or on more open-ended tasks selected by the learner • Learning to learn activities, e.g. skills practice, learning material selection, goal setting, reflection • Preparation of an oral presentation, drama or debate	• Keep learners engaged and motivated • Raise awareness of learning strategies • Give learners control of their own learning or of group sessions • Provide opportunities for giving feedback on language skills through tutors, peers and learner self-assessment
Learner log or diary	• A written record of weekly tasks and achievements (possibly with space for reflection and review) • E-logs sent to programme organisers, tutors, etc. or contributions to a discussion list • Responses to a set of reflective questions relevant to the learning sessions attended or to a personal study plan	• Encourage learners to be more reflective • Keep in contact with learners who are working mainly independently • Obtain feedback from learners on any sessions attended or learning materials used • Use as an assessment tool to measure learner independence
Learner portfolio	• The European Language Portfolio: a three part record-keeping tool for language learners which includes a **Passport** (proficiency), **Biography** (planning and reflecting) and **Dossier** (examples of achievements or work completed) • Other portfolios may have a less formal structure than the one above but have the same general aims of recording language competence, encouraging reflection and providing examples of achievements (including skills for employment)	• Help learners build a detailed record of their learning, including targets met, materials used and marks or qualifications gained • Encourage learner reflection • Use as an assessment tool for language progression and learner independence • Observe how language learning relates to other areas of the learner's experience, e.g. work, leisure, family
Attendance or participation	• Attendance at face-to-face sessions • Meetings with learning advisors • Attendance at study group sessions • Participation in video or telephone conferencing • Informal contact with teachers and other support staff • Visits to the language resource centre	• Encourage attendance at meetings • Record and follow-up drop-outs • Compare enrolment and completion numbers • Have an overview of (and input to) the learner's own learning programme • Identify problems with language, motivation, time management • Gauge how much use is made of advisors and materials that are available to learners

3.5 Evaluation

Key recommendations:
a. Use data from assessment and monitoring of learners to evaluate your programme
b. Use evaluation to revise and refine your programme

Introduction
When developing a new approach or methodology for language teaching you will need to build in an evaluative element. For a small-scale programme this will not necessarily involve an external evaluator but it will be very useful to collect data from participants (learners, teachers, partners) to assess whether your programme has achieved its aims for all those concerned. Informal feedback can be collected verbally or in writing (through questionnaires, for example) while the programme is in progress, but it is useful to have written feedback at the end (see *Photocopiable materials: Learner feedback forms*). Below are some questions that you should ask yourself when evaluating your programme.

www.opendoor2languages.net

 How will I know if what I have done has been successful?

Firstly you will need to decide what outcome you are evaluating. This may include learner progression, learner motivation or learner satisfaction with the programme as a whole.

The following table describes these in more detail:

Evaluation of	Key questions	Evidenced by
Learner progression *(see Assessment)*	Have learners made progress in their language skills?	Comparison of entry tests with exit tests Successful completion of progressive tasks or the course
	Have learners made progress as independent learners?	Learner diaries or portfolios that record planning, work completed, learning materials used, reflection on learning
	Have learners made progress as language learners?	Records or discussion of learning strategies used and reflection on the process of language learning
Learner motivation	Have learners completed tasks set by themselves and others (peers or teachers)?	Submission of work Record keeping
	Have learners completed the programme?	Attendance at formal meetings Completion of learning or assessment tasks Submission of feedback
	Have learners kept in contact with peers, organisers and teachers?	Emails, telephone calls, face-to-face meetings
Learner satisfaction	Do learners feel they have benefitted from the programme?	Feedback from ongoing dialogue (email, telephone, meetings) and end of programme questionnaires or discussions

 Was it good value for the learners?

This will be indicated by learner feedback, however, you may not want to ask this question directly but other questions relating to personal satisfaction, progress, materials, etc. should provide good indicators of this (see *Photocopiable materials: Learner feedback form*). Also you should be able to infer from good learner retention, attitude and motivation that your programme has been worthwhile for learners.

 Was it good value for the organisers?

This is somewhat harder to judge unless you have costed your programme very carefully. The following considerations will have an impact on questions of value for money:
- Is your programme subsidised or not? E.g. If your programme is entirely unsubsidised and is required to show a profit or at least break even you will be required to assess value for money in a very specific way
- What other indicators of value (non-financial) may apply? E.g. if your aim was to create links with the local community as a public service, did you achieve this?
- Was there any added value for you from your programme? E.g. did it enhance the profile of your organisation?
- Have you developed a new course or materials that can be used again commercially? E.g. can you recruit more learners or publish your course materials?

 What have been the benefits for the wider community?

If your programme was designed to meet a local or special need, or simply to bring language learning to a different group of learners you may wish to explore whether your programme has:
- Raised awareness of the benefits of language learning
- Filled a gap in local, national or international provision
- Created new partnerships
- Promoted plurilingualism (EU dimension)
- Helped sustain the teaching of minority languages
- Provided access to language learning for underprivileged groups

What has been the impact of the programme on those involved in delivering it?

As well as obtaining feedback from learners on the programme you will need to evaluate what the programme has meant for you, your organisation and your partners.

Some of the possible outcomes might be:
- Being innovative
- Reaching a new set of learners
- Opportunities for getting back into (or out of) the classroom
- Trying out a new teaching role or methodology
- Meeting new people
- Doing something useful for the community
- Becoming personally enriched
- Developing new materials
- Exploiting a wider set of materials and technologies
- Sharing problems and successes with colleagues
- Good publicity for the department or organisation involved
- Cooperation with other departments or organisations
- Meeting an educational or political agenda

3.6 Replicability and sustainability

Key recommendations:
a. Consider your programme as a template for other activities
b. Consider issues of reusability when planning and developing learning materials for your programme
c. Make your partnerships with others work for you in the long-term

Introduction
You may adopt a one-off programme designed to meet a specific set of learner needs at a specific time, e.g. a taster day to promote a set of courses or a course commissioned by a particular group. However, to make the most of the time, effort, money and expertise that you have put into designing, resourcing and delivering your programme, it is advisable to consider issues of replicability and sustainability.

Replicability

 Are the learning materials reusable?

The responses to this question will vary from programme to programme. For some it will be the idea that will be reusable, e.g. a taster day for French could be replicated with new materials for Hungarian. For other programmes the website and study pack could be reused either for the same course or to contribute to more traditional courses and learners. It is, of course, advisable to consider issues of reusability when developing materials for your programme as this will help you make the most of the considerable time and cost required to produce them.

Could I re-run the programme with new learners?

If you have developed a successful programme and a reusable set of materials, techniques or ideas then it is very likely that your programme could be run repeatedly. Equally you may wish to run it again, but in a different way, e.g. a face-to-face course could be delivered online.

 Could someone else run the programme using my ideas or materials?

The answer to this question will relate to how specific your programme was to you or to your learners. You may have needed to use several tutors to help run the programme and therefore already have some indication of how easy it is for others to use your programme. Simply adding some teacher notes to your materials may help clarify things if you are making your programme available outside of your organisation.

Sustainability

 What provision is there for continuation with the same learners?

Have you built in provision for progression? This could take the following forms:
- A second level course
- Further materials or study packs for independent learners
- Establishment of learner study groups (that you will continue to support in some way)
- Continued contact with learners through electronic means (email, website, etc.)
- Membership of your language resource centre
- Providing learning materials or study guides to your partners, e.g. the local library

 What other local provision is there for language learning?

This will help you to determine either where your learners could go to further their learning (if you are unable to provide progression) or to help you to assess the local market for language learning and to identify any gaps.

 What would be the implications of a continuation or re-run for staffing and other materials?

These are largely issues of cost and recruitment. If your programme was subsidised through a grant or other funding you may have to re-think how you run it a second time, e.g. change the contact hours, raise the fee to learners or use fewer staff. If you have already developed materials, this is an area where staff and other materials will be saved, particularly if your materials can be delivered to learners electronically rather than in hard copy. If your programme has been experimental, but successful, it may be that your organisation or your partners will take up the programme and provide the funding to sustain it.

 How can my partnerships with other organisations delivering language learning be sustained or extended?

You may find that working with other organisations leads to a successful and long-term partnership. This may simply take the form of a dialogue between (probably similar) organisations in which ideas and expertise are shared. For others, such as public and private partnerships or cross-sectoral partnerships, it may lead to other activities (not necessarily of the same type) and will provide partners with a new resource to call on in the future.

Case study 7

Professional development for university lecturers

The idea for this project was prompted by a request from Vilnius University lecturers, who give lectures and make presentations in English. The project team at the Institute of Foreign Languages designed and developed an independent learning programme, which through *activating* (presentation and discussion) sessions provided training in how to develop and improve English lecturing skills.

The learners, who were non-specialist learners of English, had regular sessions with a language teacher to discuss different issues relating to lecturing in English and to monitor their progress. There were ten activating sessions, dealing with issues such as giving academic presentations in English, differences between spoken and written language, developing academic vocabulary, handling questions, and making use of visual aids and IT in the classroom. The learners were provided with independent learner packs developed by the course team. The Institute helped the learners with the materials, and gave advice and feedback on their progress. The sessions (with the exception of the ones dealing with the use of visual aids and technology) were delivered in English. At the end of the programme the participants gave presentations in English, which were assessed by the audience and a panel of teachers.

The course participants praised the idea of the programme and noted that participation in the project boosted their confidence:

> "The most important thing about the project for me personally was **the confidence I gained**"

They also wrote about their determination to continue with the study of English after the project's completion: some of them were considering joining a language school or studying on their own. On the other hand, however, some of them noted in their feedback forms that they were not sure whether their language skills had improved.

Another important aspect of the project was the promotion of the idea of independent learning. The Lithuanian educational system is still very teacher-directed, although some considerable changes have taken place in recent years. The idea of independent learning, therefore, could benefit from further promotion at all levels of education, not only in the study of languages.

One more very important gain for the Institute of Foreign Languages and the Faculty of Philology was the change in the Institute's image - the project enabled it to offer lecturers from other faculties something very useful for free. The project has already been replicated as the University has used the model to introduce regular courses for academic staff who need support in developing their skills in lecturing in English. The course participants will be awarded certificates of professional development.

4. Learning materials

4.1 Technology

Key recommendations

a. Fit the technology to the programme, not vice versa
b. Do a technical skills audit with your learners at the start
c. Don't forget that old technologies (e.g. video, telephone) can be just as valuable as new ones (e.g. the Internet)
d. Ensure that you have made adequate provision for access to the technology that you have chosen
e. Have a back-up plan in case your technologies let you down (this can be very demotivating for learners)

Introduction

This section is about the different technologies you may wish to use when running an open learning programme. (For more details about the nature and application of particular technologies see *Appendix 3: Technologies for language learning*). Once you have developed your ideas and decided what kind of programme you want to run, you will be faced with a number of issues in terms of selecting technologies, such as cost implications and availability. The following are some of the questions that may arise.

 What technologies are most appropriate to the planned programme?

For example, in a distance e-learning model, you and your learners will need a reliable Internet connection; for an open access programme your organisation will need technologies such as video and audio facilities, personal computers and Internet connections to be available in the library or language resource centre. Try to anticipate problems (access, skills and appropriateness) and identify clearly which technologies you will need. Examine whether you are able to supply these technologies and if not, what level of technologies you should or could expect learners to have access to.

 How can the use of the selected technology add value?

Technology will add value to your programme if it makes learning more interesting, more accessible, and more flexible. For example, it will be very useful if you are able to offer additional exercises or materials on a website. However, for anything other than an e-learning course, you should be cautious about using too much technology: bear in mind that your programme is not about technology but mainly about languages. People may be put off if too much technology or too many technical skills are required.

What will be the role of communication technology in my programme?

Communication technology will facilitate contact between the teacher and learners, and also between the learners themselves. Such technologies include email, discussion lists and chat rooms. Don't forget that the telephone (mobile and landlines) is a very cheap and widespread means of communication. SMS text messaging has also become a very effective way of both sending messages and delivering short learning activities.

 What IT skills will learners need to access learning?

It is advisable to be very clear about what IT skills are required to participate in the programme. This way you will avoid problems for yourself and disappointment for your learners. Also, do not take anything for granted: check with your learners whether they have the required IT skills, even if you consider these very basic or simple.

 What technologies will be available to learners and where?

Although modern technologies are becoming increasingly accessible, many people still do not have access to technologies such as the Internet or email at home. An alternative solution for these people could be making the technology available in your organisation, for example at an agreed time. This is extremely useful if you are working with a specific software package: you can send the tool to all those with a computer so they can install it (copyright permitting), and you can also make it available in your own organisation. If opening access to your own organisation is impossible, you might think of working with a public centre, such as a community centre, or you could try to negotiate cheap access for your learners at an Internet centre.

Case study 8

Virtual conversation

This programme concentrated on using video and telephone conferencing for conversation practice in Spanish. It aimed to give learners the opportunity to practise conversation when face-to-face meetings were difficult or impossible. It also provided the opportunity to meet and converse with native speakers and introduced learners to a new technology for language learning.

The programme was developed in Sweden by the Alléskolan adult education unit in partnership with the National Agency for Flexible Learning (CFL) as part of an interactive web-based course where opportunities for face-to-face oral conversation were lacking. It involved two different ways of using new media in conversation.

The video conferencing model involved learners with some knowledge of Spanish, who wanted conversation practice. As they lived far apart, it was difficult for them to meet face-to-face. The video conferencing sessions were held at four resource centres in the region, including Alléskolan. The sessions ran for two hours, once a fortnight, and were led by a native Spanish teacher from Alléskolan. The participants were given a set of themes in advance, which enabled them to prepare for conversations about life in Sweden, Swedish culture, and comparisons between Sweden and Spain. For the final session, the whole group met face-to-face at Alléskolan, where they were shown a Spanish film and shared some food.

The telephone conference model was designed for students taking part in a distance learning course at CFL, who lacked speaking opportunities. Learners were offered five conversation sessions at a time of their choosing. As with the video conferencing group, they were given a set of themes to enable them to prepare for the sessions. The themes were chosen to encourage them to talk about everyday life and there were also role-plays adapted for the telephone. Two students and a native speaker were connected for a three-way conversation lasting about half an hour. The teacher listened and gave feedback after the sessions.

Many non-traditional language learners like the flexibility of distance learning but they often miss out on speaking practice. The evaluations from the test show that video and telephone can be an effective way of providing an oral element for distance learners.

The retention rate for the test was very good and the participants enjoyed the informal atmosphere. Learners came well prepared and took an active part in conversation, overcoming the initial embarrassment of using the technology. An important factor was the native speaker who made the sessions more authentic. The participants appreciated the themes chosen, and they felt more confident about speaking when they had been able to prepare topics in advance.

> "It was useful to **have a teacher who has Spanish as her native language**.
> It makes it more difficult to lapse into Swedish when you want to try to explain something in stumbling Spanish. It was also very interesting to get information about life in Cuba."

What was also interesting for the organisers was the comparison between the use of the telephone which is the most accessible and cheapest medium and videoconferencing which gives better opportunities for authentic conversation but is less flexible as it requires access to up-to-date technology and much more forward planning.

4.2 Study packs and published materials

Key recommendations

a. Ensure that your programme provides opportunities to experience a wide range of language learning materials but be aware that learners can be overwhelmed by too much choice

b. Be sure that your programme offers adequate access to learning materials. If you cannot offer these, explore the establishment of a partnership with an organisation that can, e.g. a library, language resource centre, or a publisher.

c. Provide guidance on available learning materials and suggestions for how to get the best use out of them

Introduction

Learning materials are, of course, a key element of any language learning programme. Having considered the target group and its needs you will need to identify appropriate materials that you will either develop yourself or select from a range of published materials. Whichever you choose, giving your learners a study pack will help to guide their learning, provide exercises at the correct level or serve as a record-keeping tool.

 What is meant by study packs?

These are some of the different types of study packs that might be offered to learners, together with a brief definition and an explanation of their use in open learning programmes:

Language learning materials: these encompass any material that is either explicitly intended for language learning (e.g. textbooks, interactive computer exercises, audiotapes) or authentic material that can be used for language learning (e.g. newspapers, websites, television programmes, songs, etc). The latter may need adapting for learning by the addition of activities, glossaries or translations.

Learning guides will usually give advice to learners on how to improve their language learning skills. They may include advice on language learning strategies and activities to help learners become more reflective. They may also include templates for planning learning, self-assessment and recording progress (see *Record-keeping tools below*).

Resource guides may also be included in either of the packs above and are intended to provide information on the types of materials available and advice on how they may be used by learners. They may also contain suggestions for activities that learners can use to get the best out of a particular type of learning material.

In-house course materials are usually prepared for a particular organisation, company, or group, e.g. university students. They are usually part of closed courses, and may be delivered electronically or in printed form.

Published courses may be for self-study or for classroom use and can be purchased by learners, or offered in a library or language resource centre. They will give learners a learning path and learning activities, and are available for a variety of levels. They are usually sequential in structure and can be used as a core course book or offered as support material (for grammar exercises, revision, grammar help).

Record-keeping tools help learners to assess their progress as learners, and allow tutors to monitor learning and progress in the language. An example of such a tool is the European Language Portfolio (see *Monitoring*).

The following are some questions that you will need to discuss with the staff involved in developing the content of your programme.

 ### Will a study pack be needed?

Working with non-traditional or non-specialist language learners, especially within an open learning context relying on autonomy and self-motivation, it is likely that the support provided by a study pack will be essential. Study packs are key motivators, they provide the learner with something tangible to take away, and they help learners to develop organisational skills. Which pack to choose will depend on the kind of programme developed, its aims and objectives and the needs of learners. There is such a wealth of material available for language learning that it is easy for learners to become overwhelmed by choice, thus a study pack or course book will give them a secure and manageable starting point, from which they can explore the wider range of materials as their confidence and competence develops. Examples of study packs can be found on the OdLL Project website: www.opendoor2languages.net

 ### Will the study packs be produced in-house, or will published materials be used?

Although there is a very wide variety of language learning materials available, they may not be appropriate for your learners, e.g. not appropriate for self-study, or too difficult to use without help (in the case of authentic materials). Teachers may choose to adapt or select from a range of published materials or even develop their own. It might, however, be useful to provide learners with a traditional course book or a printed textbook, as very often learners find it difficult to adjust to non-traditional methods, therefore a partially traditional approach could put them at ease.

 ### What range of materials will be used and how will they be selected?

The range of language learning materials currently available (especially for languages such as English, French, Spanish and German) is very wide and covers a variety of media. Where learners are working largely autonomously there are particular challenges:

Access - where and when can learners gain access to materials? Do they have to use them in a learning resource centre or can they take them home? Are they online or in printed form?

Quantity - how to assist learners to select appropriate materials from the wide range available at different levels? There is currently something of a shift towards digital materials (CD-ROM, DVD, Internet) for language learning, but there is still plenty of scope for the use of old technologies (books, audiotapes, video) as these are cheap, easy to use and less reliant on expensive hardware.

Learning activities - do the materials have in-built learning activities (e.g. course books) or do learners need guidance on how to use materials (e.g. authentic materials such as films, newspapers, etc)? The latter can be provided either by writing learning activities that relate to a particular authentic material or by providing advice on how to use different types of authentic material for learning, e.g. techniques for learning from the news.

 ### Will the choice of materials be left to the learners?

It is a good idea to encourage learners to choose their own materials and to share their favourites with fellow learners. They will often discover materials their teachers do not know about or will favour a particular type of material that is adapted for self-study. However, for the reasons given above, learners should always have access to advice (from a teacher or a printed guide).

What are the copyright implications of using commercial or authentic materials in a study pack?

Reproducing published materials in study packs should be undertaken in line with local copyright laws. Anything that is reproduced should acknowledge the source and nothing should be reproduced for commercial use without permission from the original author.

 Is the purchase of additional materials necessary?

If your programme is allowing a free choice of languages, using a particular medium (e.g. the computer) or concentrating on a type of material (e.g. films) this may necessitate the purchase of additional materials. This needs to be taken into account at the planning stage and conducting an inventory of your and your partner's materials will help to determine how open and flexible your programme can be. If you wish to use a published course book you may need to include the cost of this in the price of your programme.

Case study 9

Learner training for independent language learners

ReActivate your language learning was a learner training programme for adult learners in the United Kingdom who wanted to refresh a language and to study in more informal, independent and flexible ways. It aimed to help learners identify and set their language learning goals and to develop a better range of language learning strategies. It also gave guidance on how to get the best out of the learning materials available.

The programme consisted of six face-to face sessions at Southampton Central Library and six study group meetings with a native speaker. In an initial session, learners were invited to reflect on their past learning experiences and write their language biography. In later sessions learners used a simplified version of the Common European Framework to self-assess and they were shown the Dialang system for online assessment. They also discussed their reasons for wanting to learn a language and looked at their individual learning styles. Additionally, learners were introduced to a wide variety of learning materials available in the library and on the Internet, they were given language exercises and invited to consider the strategies they were using in order to complete the tasks. Learners were then left to continue their language study on their own and through the study groups, facilitated by a native speaker, which helped give oral practice (a skill it is hard to develop alone) and to maintain motivation.

Support materials consisted of a learner handbook and a website.

This method of learner training, combined with study group work with native speakers, appeared popular with learners:

"I realised just how much there is out there **to help you**"

"It gives you the confidence that you **can motivate yourself**"

"I have definitely realised that **I learn best by listening**"

The online programme booklet and the website (www.opendoor2languages.net/reactivate) make it reasonably easy to replicate the programme, which can be completed by learners (on their own) or delivered by a teacher. It is the case, however, that the most challenging aspect of the programme for learners to achieve on their own is the setting up of a study group with a native speaker.

www.opendoor2languages.net

5. Summary of key recommendations

Why develop an open learning programme?	Don't reinvent the wheel - use and adapt existing programmes, planning checklists, feedback and evaluation forms, etc.
	Build in systems for learner assessment, monitoring, and feedback
	Consider questions of costs and long term viability
	Be aware that unforeseen problems will arise, so be flexible and remember that your programme is learner-centred
Assessing learner needs and goals	The earlier you find out what learners want, the better
	Rely mainly on a written questionnaire to collect your data
	Make the questionnaire as convenient for the learner as possible by using mostly closed question types but give the learner a chance to add extra information with at least one open question
	Be flexible and able to adapt to learner needs
Selecting a model	Design a programme that combines three key elements: learner training, access to learning materials and access to a support network of fellow learners, teachers or native speakers
	Be aware of existing local provision for language learning
Funding	Ask your learners to pay a fee (free is not always interpreted as good)
	Work with other organisations to help spread the cost
Publicity and recruitment	Allow plenty of time to recruit learners
	Don't rely solely on leaflets and posters
	Use advertisements in local newspapers where possible. A tight budget need not be a limitation as some publications allow you to advertise for free.
	Ensure that your publicity is clear about exactly what is on offer, what learning is expected and who is eligible to participate
Setting a timetable	Consider the profile of your learners (age, employment status, geographical situation, etc.) when selecting the timing for your activities
	Don't run your programme during the summer vacation period
Selecting a venue	Identify which type of facilities your model will require. If possible, try organising the programme using your own facilities; if not, look for alternative solutions.
	Be prepared to pay a fee to use external facilities and book well in advance
	Try to give your learners access to a resource centre but be aware that they may prefer or need to work at home
Staff	Determine whether you are able to employ all required staff before you start the programme
	Use staff with a variety of competences
	Try to use native speakers and language students in your programme, where appropriate
Cooperation with others	Find partners with skills, expertise and facilities to complement your own and offer them something in return
	Don't work with too many partners
	Liaise with a particular person rather than an organisation and keep in regular contact
	Set clear goals and an exact timetable to avoid misunderstandings

Learner support	Be aware of the multiple roles that a teacher can adopt, e.g. facilitator, counsellor or resource
	Start with a learner needs analysis
	Bear in mind what the learners want and can do
	Keep in contact with learners
Motivation	Be clear about what your programme is offering
	Give support to learners (online or face-to-face) especially at the beginning
	Introduce an incentive, e.g. charge a fee to be reimbursed at the end or offer a certificate
Assessment	Don't assess for its own sake (take account of what learners need or want)
	Develop assessment to fit the programme offered
	Have clear learning outcomes (organiser or learner defined) to guide your choice of assessment
Monitoring	Incorporate systems for maintaining records of learning and attendance
	Ensure that communication is maintained with learners especially when they are working independently
	Record learner profiles and collect feedback on the programme
Evaluation	Use data from assessment and monitoring of learners to evaluate your programme
	Use evaluation to revise and refine your programme
Replicability and sustainability	Consider your programme as a template for other activities
	Consider issues of reusability when planning and developing learning materials for your programme
	Make your partnerships with others work for you in the long-term
Technology	Fit the technology to the model, not vice versa
	Do a technical skills audit with your learners at the start
	Don't forget that old technologies (e.g. video, telephone) can be just as valuable as new ones (e.g. the Internet)
	Ensure that you have made adequate provision for access to the technology that you have chosen
	Have a back-up plan in case your technologies let you down (this can be very demotivating for learners)
Study packs and published materials	Ensure that your programme provides opportunities to experience a wide range of language learning materials but be aware that learners can be overwhelmed by too much choice
	Be sure that your programme offers adequate access to learning materials. If you cannot offer these, explore the establishment of a partnership with an organisation that can, e.g. a library, language resource centre, or a publisher.
	Provide guidance on available learning materials and suggestions for how to get the best use out of them

Appendix 1: Types of independent language learning

Type of Independent Language Learning (ILL)	Place or location	Materials	Professional support	Learner type
1. Autodidaxy Not directed Not supported Solitary	Independent of educational environments Distance irrelevant	Self resourced (e.g. builds own materials from newspapers or television)	None, self-resourced (but uses people for practice)	Probably does not exist outside of polyglots
2. Self-study Rarely supported Normally solo Self-reliant	Learning location immaterial (home, train, bus, jogging)	Teach-yourself packages Broadcast courses Dictionaries Grammars	None or episodic Operates alone	Hopes that knowledge is found in a book, and can then be applied to the outside world. Learner is isolated. Treats learning as a self-contained package. Has problems developing speaking skills.
3. Open learning May be part directed and supported	Dependent upon a facility offering open access to materials and advice	Selects eclectically from a range of materials, preferably open access	Takes advice widely from librarians, advisors, teachers, but not systematically	Likes to browse and talk to others. Finds the human environment as useful as its physical contents. Some planning involved.
4. Supported independent learning Always supported May operate at distance	Relies (initially, sometimes continually) upon institutional materials, especially people	Teach-yourself packages Broadcast courses Textbooks Dictionaries Grammars Self-study packs	Systematic use of: Advisors Study groups Tandem learning partners Classes Meetings	Accepts that others may have the solution to their needs, but basically wants to operate independently

David Bickerton (OdLL Project Evaluator, 2003)

Appendix 2: The profile of learners participating in the OdLL Project 2002-2005

This appendix provides a general profile of the learners who participated in the Opening the Door to Language Learning Project in the seven partner countries (Belgium, Hungary, Ireland, Lithuania, Spain, Sweden and the United Kingdom). This data is compiled from information provided by participants in the second phase of the OdLL Project.

Age groups

This graph summarises data for all partner countries. Altogether 156 participants were involved in the phase two tests. The 25-34 age group was the best represented (49 participants). The smallest group (5) were people over 65. A large number of learners were between 35 and 54: 67 learners divided almost evenly between these two categories.

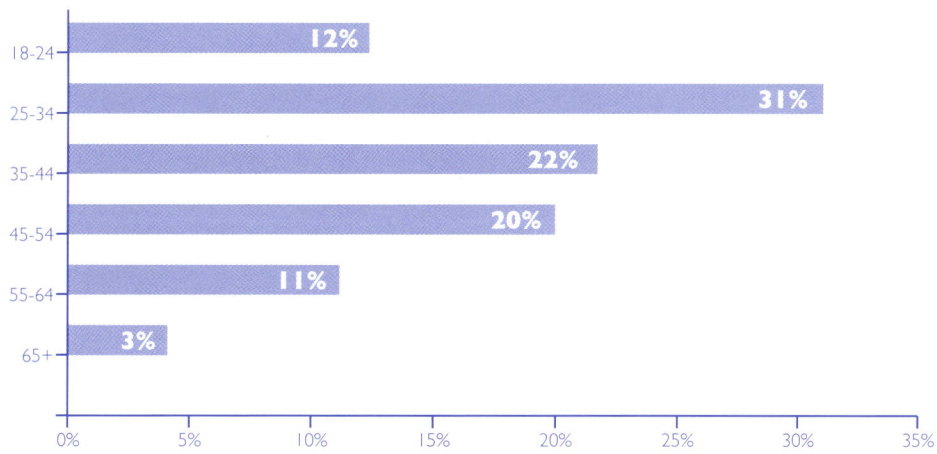

Gender

105 participants were female (67%), 51 were male (33%).

Educational experience

Almost all participants (126) reported secondary education experience. A large number (86) had higher or university education experience. A quarter of the group had postgraduate and adult education experience (40 and 36 people respectively). A small group had previously participated in evening classes.

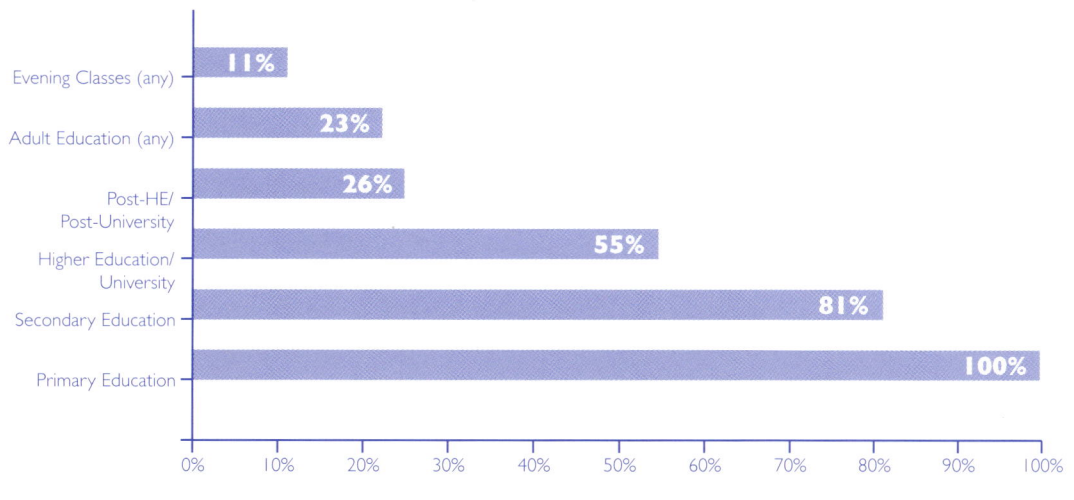

Language learning goals

In phase two, OdLL Project partners asked participants about their language learning goals. These goals and the percentage of participants who selected them are listed in the table below. On the learner profile form (see *Photocopiable materials: Learner profile form*) learners were asked to tick boxes next to the goals that were applicable to them. Learners also had the opportunity to add additional goals - these are indicated by brackets in the table.

We then classifed these goals into four types: Non-Specific type (NS); Skills type (SK); Functional type (FU) and Social type (SO). This is shown in the third column.

I want to be able to read books, papers and magazines in this language	44.9 %	SK
I want to be able to use this language when I'm on holiday	42.3 %	FU
I have studied the language and want to refresh my knowledge	41.7 %	NS
I want to be able to watch TV and listen to the radio in this language	37.8 %	SK
I want to be able to use this language in letters or emails	36.8 %	SK/SO
I just like to study languages	35.9 %	NS
For professional purposes	35.3 %	FU
I like the country where this language is spoken	34.6 %	NS
In order to meet other people and socialise	30.8 %	SO
I am interested in developing a greater degree of independence in my learning	26.9 %	SK
I want to live or work where the language is spoken	16.0 %	FU
I am looking for a good way to use my free time	15.4 %	NS
I have relatives in or from the country where this language is spoken	5.1 %	FU/SO
(I want to help my children with their homework)	5.1 %	FU
I have been advised to improve my language skills by my employer	1.3 %	FU
I have a holiday home in the country where the language is spoken	1.3 %	FU
(Flamenco is a passion, I want to understand the lyrics)	0.6 %	SK
(I just love the language)	0.6 %	NS
(I want to learn some new strategies for language learning)	0.6 %	NS
(I want to study Celtic history and mythology)	0.6 %	FU
(I want to get advice on lecturing in English)	0.6 %	NS
(Pronunciation is poor, I want to improve this)	0.6 %	SK

OdLL learners' responses to closed questions

Overall, and in almost every single OdLL Project country, "I want to be able to read books, papers and magazines in the language" was the most popular answer. Clearly, reading ability in the target language is a high priority across the continent. Other skill-centred answers (such as "I want to be able to use this language in letters or emails" and "I want to be able to watch TV and listen to the radio in this language", dealing with writing and listening, respectively) were also popular.

Learners in pre-defined groups often share the same goals. In Lithuania, for example, all twenty phase two learners ticked one particular answer. And given that the Lithuanian programme offered in-service training, it is not surprising that the answer they all selected was "For professional purposes." Overall, this answer was the seventh most popular.

Given the emphasis on independent learning throughout the OdLL Project, it is noteworthy that only in Hungary, which targetted hearing-impaired learners was "I am interested in developing a greater degree of independence in my learning" the most popular option. Perhaps the additional challenges faced by hearing-impaired learners provide an explanation for their concern with autonomy.

Examples of answers OdLL learners gave to open questions

In Limerick, Ireland, no fewer than eight out of twelve phase two learners mentioned travelling to France as a reason for learning French. In Maynooth, Ireland, learners mentioned "culture", "national identity", "self-improvement" and "personal development" as reasons for learning Irish.

Responses given by United Kingdom phase one learners indicated the following goals:
- To live abroad. A number of learners had bought or were considering buying property in the target language country.
- To develop 'everyday' language to be able to communicate when on holiday
- To develop business language to enhance professional lives and job prospects
- To help children with homework
- To learn more about the culture of the target language country
- For pleasure or the challenge of learning a new language
- To improve grammar and vocabulary
- To develop listening, reading, speaking or writing skills
- To learn through online and audio-visual means rather than book-related study
- To find an effective way to maintain a language acquired in an adult education course

In contrast to such a diverse range of motives, phase two learners in Lithuania were concerned exclusively with professional self-development. They mentioned improving "fluency in academic discourse" and "skills of scientific communication" and referred to "the structure and features of a lecture" in their open responses. As has already been mentioned there were clear reasons for this being the case.

Cultural reasons were cited in Belgium, with Tango, Flamenco and song lyrics being mentioned, and one learner wanted "to be able to express my opinion to Spanish poets or writers whenever they come to Antwerp."

Spanish learners of English were keen to be able to help their children with homework, and in Sweden, one learner with some enforced free time (in prison) wanted "to learn something useful."

www.opendoor2languages.net

Appendix 3: Technologies for language learning

Type	Description	What is it good for?	Models	Examples
Audio-visual technology	Including TV, DVD, VCR, CDs and CD-players, multimedia equipment, digital photography, tape players and recorders, video cameras, overhead projectors	Making learning more exciting and authentic. It can help learners to develop their listening skills (audio, video, film) and to improve their production skills (creating materials using camera equipment). In addition, it allows teachers to organise activities that they cannot always find time for in class time (e.g. film shows, cultural events).	Open access Roadshow Study or conversation group	Open learning models 2, 4, 5 Case study 5: Creating social conditions for language learning Case study 6: Using drama to motivate learners
Chat rooms (synchronous conversation)	This Internet application allows two or more people to communicate using short written messages	Best for informal learning between peers but can provide a good alternative to face-to-face advice sessions between learners and teachers. Could be used by tandem learners for real time conversation (see also *Discussion lists and Email* below). Some chat software allows file transfer thus allowing learning activities to be shared remotely.	Open access Study or conversation group	Open learning model 4: Open access
Computer software	CD-ROMs, Computer Assisted Language Learning (CALL) software, language processing tools, e.g. concordancers, translation software	Offers multimedia-learning material, which can be more dynamic than a printed course. Can be made available in a fixed location, e.g. resource centre or library. Because this is often tied to a particular computer or server, and for copyright reasons, it cannot always be delivered remotely to learners.	Open access Roadshow Taster days	Open learning model 4: Open access Case study 2: Language roadshow
Discussion lists (Mainly asynchronous)	Web-based forum on which people can post and read messages	Suitable for language advising. Also could be used by study groups whereby learners can interact informally or discuss a topic they or the facilitator/teacher have chosen. Unlike email, messages are visible to everyone in the group and remain on the website.	Distance learning (via a virtual learning environment or the Internet) Virtual language advising	Open learning models 1, 6 Case study 4: Language advice service for parents
Email (Mainly asynchronous)	Including free web-based mail as well as locally-managed mail	An excellent and simple means of communicating with and between learners. Can be used to create communities of learners (as above) and for e-tandem learning (conversation exchange). Materials can be sent to or exchanged by learners. Also very useful for giving language learning advice.	Distance learning Study or conversation group	Open learning models 1, 2 Case study 1: Supporting language learners with special needs
Internet	Could involve the use of an external website or a site developed for a particular organisation or learning programme. Portals and gateways also offer collections of links to sources of cultural or learning material.	For designing and delivering online courses, materials and exercises that will be accessible from everywhere. Also a good way to refer to additional, third party materials and authentic materials. When using an intranet or website managed by the host organisation it is possible to restrict access to learners enrolled on a particular learning programme.	Distance learning Learner training Open access	Open learning models 1, 3, 4 Case study 9: Learner training for independent language learners
Telephone	Includes landline and mobile telephone, SMS text messaging	Establishing contact between learners and teachers, advisors, etc. especially where they are in diverse or remote locations. Could be used for advice and as an alternative to face-to-face sessions. Also for oral and aural exercises.	Language Advising Study or conversation group	Open learning models 2, 6 Case study 8: Virtual conversation
Video conferencing	Equipment used for establishing video connection between two or more organisations (Ethernet connections or web cam)	Establishing face-to-face contact between learners and teachers within and between countries. People are able to see one another, which helps to create a community of learners and makes interaction more authentic. Technical problems can be frustrating, however.	Language Advising Study or conversation group	Open learning models 2, 6 Case study 8: Virtual conversation
Virtual learning environment	Web-based system for creating and distributing learning materials. Often also offers student tracking and discussion forum.	Allows tutors to create and deliver structured online courses or give support in a restricted (students only) environment. Use can be tracked, discussion groups set up, and weekly tasks delivered.	Distance and e-learning	Open learning model 1: Distance learning

52 **Appendices**

Photocopiable materials

Checklist for designing an open learning model

This checklist was used for designing the open learning tests outlined in the table of models (*See Table 1: Open learning models*). A version of the checklist with space for entering your own planned activities is downloadable from the OdLL Project website: www.opendoor2languages.net

Ask yourself	Chapter reference	Actions	Dates (start, end)	Persons involved	Time input	Costs
Planning and practicalities						
Why develop an open learning programme? Why am I doing this?	2.1					
Assessing learner needs and goals What do learners want or need?	2.2					
Selecting a model What will I offer?	2.3					
Funding How will I fund it?	2.4					
Publicity and recruitment How will I recruit learners?	2.5					
Languages What language(s) will I offer?	2.6					
Setting a timetable How will I organise the programme?	2.7					
Selecting a venue Where will I run it?	2.8					
Staff What staff do I need?	2.9					
Cooperation with others Who will I be working with?	2.10					
Pedagogic issues						
Learner support What support will I give to learners?	3.1					
Motivation How will I motivate learners?	3.2					
Assessment How will I assess learners?	3.3					
Monitoring How will I monitor learners?	3.4					
Evaluation How will I evaluate the model?	3.5					
Replicability and sustainability How will I replicate or sustain the model?	3.6					
Learning materials						
Technology What technology will I use?	4.1					
Study packs and published materials What learning materials will I use or develop?	4.2					

Learner profile form

The information you provide in this form is for internal use only and will not be passed on to third parties. It will help us to decide if this programme is right for you and will also help us to develop the programme to meet your needs.

Contact details

Name: ....

Address: ....

....

City or town: ....

Postcode: ....

Daytime telephone number: ....

Mobile number: ....

Email: ....

About you

Which age group are you in?

    ❏ 18-24   ❏ 25-34   ❏ 35-44   ❏ 45-54   ❏ 55-64   ❏ 65+

Are you   ❏ Male?   ❏ Female?

What is your current occupation? (please specify): ....
(This includes homemaker, student, carer, retired, etc.)

If not currently working, what was your previous occupation? ....

Educational experience - not necessarily in languages (please tick all boxes that apply):

    ❏ Further Education or Adult Education
    ❏ University or College of Higher Education
    ❏ Postgraduate

Your language learning background

What language learning experience do you have? (include any qualifications you have): ....

....

....

....

What is your native or first language? ....

What language would you like to learn or improve? ....

Are you currently receiving formal tuition in this language?   ❏ Yes   ❏ No

What other languages do you know? Below is a simplified version of the Common European Framework for languages. Try to match your skills in all the languages you have some knowledge of (apart from your native or first language) to this framework.

Description	Languages
I am in the very early stages of learning this language. I can understand and produce some simple short sentences that relate to my personal situation. I can recognise a few words.	
I am developing the ability to communicate basic information about myself, my family and my job and can cope with simple transactions, e.g. buying train tickets.	
I am becoming able to understand the gist of longer pieces of written or spoken language, e.g. menus, timetables, posters. In conversations I can form my own sentences relating to familiar topics (myself, family, etc.) and give some basic opinions or descriptions.	
I am reaching a stage in my language learning whereby I can follow more complicated speech, e.g. a line of argument and can cope with language that relates to topical as well as personal subjects.	
I now consider myself to be a very competent user of the language. I can cope effortlessly with most situations and can express myself fluently in both social and professional contexts.	
I would describe myself as a near-native speaker of the language. I can follow fast and unedited speech and produce spoken and written language that is very well structured and can make a logical, convincing argument on any topic.	

Why do you want to study a language? (You may tick more than one box)

❏ I just like to study languages
❏ I have studied the language and want to refresh my knowledge
❏ I am interested in developing a greater degree of independence in my learning
❏ I have been advised to improve my language skills by my employer
❏ I like the country where this language is spoken
❏ In order to meet other people and socialise
❏ I have relatives in or from the country where this language is spoken
❏ I want to be able to use this language when I am on holiday
❏ I want to be able to read books, papers and magazines in this language
❏ I want to be able to use this language in letters or emails
❏ I want to be able to watch TV and listen to the radio in this language
❏ I want to live or work where the language is spoken
❏ I am looking for a good way to use my free time
❏ I have a holiday home in the country where the language is spoken
❏ For professional purposes
❏ Other: please specify

Why do you want to take part in this programme?

. . . .

. . . .

Do you have any computer skills? Please give details below

. . . .

. . . .

I have access to a personal computer: ❏ Yes   ❏ No
I have access to an Internet connection: ❏ Yes   ❏ No

Setting goals for language learning

Reflect:

Think about what you can actually achieve in the time you have available to you for your learning. If you have a long-term aim that will take some time and a lot of work to achieve, try to set smaller achievable goals along the way.

Consider:

a) What are your long-term language learning goals? What do you want to do with your chosen language(s) (e.g. write emails, travel, talk on the telephone, read books)?

I want to be able to

. . . .

. . . .

. . . .

. . . .

. . . .

b) What are your immediate goals?

My immediate goals are

. . . .

. . . .

. . . .

. . . .

. . . .

c) How much time are you planning to set aside (e.g. daily, weekly) to achieve your aims?

. . . .

. . . .

. . . .

. . . .

. . . .

Plan:

Use the grid below to help you plan your learning. Note you can have as many or as few goals as you like.

No.	Goal What do you want to achieve?	Study plan How are you going to achieve it?	Deadline When do you want to achieve it?
1.			
2.			
3.			
4.			
5.			
6.			
7.			
8.			
9.			
10.			

Learner self-assessment form

Language studied: ....

Use this form to help you to think about how you are progressing in your learning and how to keep going!

Language

1. What are you particularly enjoying and why?

   ....

   ....

2. How are you assessing your progress?

   ....

   ....

3. Are you having any particular difficulties with the language?

   ....

   ....

4. Do you feel that you have achieved your goals so far?   ❑ Yes   ❑ No

5. Do you agree with the following statements?

	Yes	No
I enjoy the freedom to study when I want to		
I enjoy being able to follow my own interests		
I like working on my own		
I am discovering new things about the way I learn		
I am a better language learner		
I feel that I am making progress in the language		
I am more confident in my ability to learn and use the language		
I tend to work on skills or activities that I am good at		
I need other people to encourage or help me		
I don't have enough time for my language learning		
I am overwhelmed by the choice of materials		
I am finding it hard to get speaking practice		
I find it hard to set myself goals		
I get demotivated very easily		

If you mainly answered yes in the top section you are clearly getting on well. If you are answering mainly yes in the bottom section think about what you need to do to address the problems you are having.

6. What steps can you take to address these difficulties?

   ....

   ....

   ....

Learning materials (books, tapes, computer software, Internet, etc.)

7. Are there any learning materials that you have found particularly useful or interesting?

....

....

8. Have you had any problems finding suitable materials?

....

....

9. What additional materials would you like to use?

....

....

Skills and strategies

10. What is your strongest skill in the language? (you may have more than one)

Reading	Writing	Listening	Speaking	Grammar	Vocabulary

11. What skill do you most need or wish to improve? (you may have more than one)

Reading	Writing	Listening	Speaking	Grammar	Vocabulary

12. How do you plan to go about improving your chosen skill(s)?

Skill	Strategies for improvement

13. What are you gaining personally from learning in this way, e.g. greater confidence in your abilities?

....

....

14. What suits you about this method of learning?

....

....

15. What doesn't suit you about this method of learning?

....

....

Next steps

16. How do you plan to continue with your learning (here are some examples but feel free to add your own)? Don't forget your original goals!

Carry on learning independently	
Be more disciplined about studying regularly	
Join a class	
Find or set up a study group	
Find a tandem (conversation exchange) partner	
Look for ways to assess my progress	
Find a personal tutor	
Visit the country where the language is spoken	
Take an intensive course	
Use a wider variety of materials	
Concentrate on improving my weakest skills	

17. Other plans

. . . .

. . . .

. . . .

. . . .

. . . .

. . . .

. . . .

. . . .

. . . .

. . . .

. . . .

. . . .

. . . .

. . . .

. . . .

. . . .

. . . .

. . . .

Learner feedback form

Name: . . . . **Date:** . . . .

Language studied . . . .

Please comment on the following areas:

The language

1. What do you feel you have gained from this experience in terms of your language learning?

    . . . .

    . . . .

2. What have you particularly enjoyed and why? . . . .

    . . . .

3. Would you say that you have made progress and in what areas? . . . .

    . . . .

4. Have you had any particular difficulties with the language? . . . .

    . . . .

5. Do you feel that you have achieved your goals?   ❑ Yes ❑ No

6. Are there any learning materials that you have found particularly useful or interesting?

    . . . .

    . . . .

The programme

7. Have you had any problems with this programme finding materials, working on your own, etc?

    . . . .

    . . . .

8. Do you feel that you have had adequate support? . . . .

    . . . .

9. Was there anything that you would have liked to have done but were unable to? . . . .

    . . . .

    . . . .

10. What have you gained personally from this programme, e.g. greater confidence in your abilities?

    . . . .

    . . . .

The future

11. Are you planning to continue with your language learning and in what way?

. . . .

. . . .

. . . .

. . . .

Any other comments

. . . .

. . . .

. . . .

. . . .

. . . .

. . . .

. . . .

How would you rate:

	Excellent	Very good	Good	Satisfactory	Unsatisfactory
The programme					
Your progress					
The facilities					
Learning materials (books, videos, computer software, etc.)					
Support (materials or people)					
Access times (if relevant)					